PRIAPUS AND THE POOL
and Other Poems

PRIAPUS
AND THE POOL

And Other Poems

By

CONRAD AIKEN

NEW YORK

BONI & LIVERIGHT

1925

To
MY WIFE

CONTENTS

PRIAPUS AND THE POOL
and Other Poems

SAMADHI

Take then the music; plunge in the thickest of it,—
Thickest, darkest, richest; call it a forest,
A million boles of trees, with leaves, leaves,
Golden and green, flashing like scales in the sun,
Tossed and torn in the tempest, whirling and
     streaming,
With the terrible sound, beneath, of boughs that
    crack.
. . . Again, a hush comes; and the wind's a
    whisper.
One leaf goes pirouetting. You stand in the dusk
In the misty shaft of light the sun flings faintly
Through planes of green; and suddenly, out of the
    darkest
And deepest and farthest of the forest, wavers
That golden horn, *cor anglais*, husky-timbred,
Sending through all this gloom of trees and silence
Its faint half-mute nostalgia. . . . How the soul
Flies from the dungeon of you to the very portals
To meet that sound! There, there, is the secret
Singing out of the darkness,—shining, too,
For all we know, if we could only see!

But if we steal by footpaths, warily,—
Snap not a twig, nor crush a single leaf;
Or if, in a kind of panic, like wild beasts,
We rend our violent way through vines and briars,
Crash through a coppice, tear our flesh, come
    bleeding
To a still pool, encircled, brooded over
By ancient trees—all's one! We reach but silence,
We find no horn, no hornsman. . . . There the
    beeches
Out of the lower dark of ferns and mosses
Lift, far above, their tremulous tops to the light.
Only an echo hear we of that horn,
Cor anglais, golden, husky-timbred, crying
Half-mute nostalgia from the dark of things. . . .
Then, as we stand bewildered in that wood,
With leaves above us in sibilant confusion,
And the ancient ghosts of leaves about our feet—
Listen!—the horn once more, but farther now,
Sings in the evening for a wing-beat space;
Makes the leaves murmur, as it makes the blood
Burn in the heart and all its radiant veins;
And we turn inward, to seek it once again.

Or, it's a morning in the blue portal of summer.
White shoals of little clouds, like heavenly fish,
Swim softly off the sun, who rains his light

SAMADHI

On the vast hurrying earth.   The giant poplar
Sings in the light with a thousand sensitive leaves,
Root-tip to leaf-tip he is all delight:
And, at the golden core of all that joy,
One sinister grackle with a thievish eye
Scrapes a harsh cynic comment.   How he laughs,
Flaunting amid that green his coffin-colour!
We, in the garden a million miles below him,
At paltry tasks of pruning, spading, watching
Black-stripèd bees crawl into foxglove bells
Half-filled with dew—look! we are lightly startled
By sense or sound; are moved; lose touch with
        earth;
And, in the twinkling of the grackle's eye,
Swing in the infinite on a spider's cable.
What is our world?   It is a poplar tree
Immense and solitary, with leaves a thousand,
Or million, countless, flashing in a light
For them alone intended.   He is great,
His trunk is solid, and his roots deceive us.
We shade our eyes with hands and upward look
To see if all those leaves indeed be leaves,
So rich they are in a choiring down of joy,
Or stars.   And as we stand so, small and dumb,
We hear again that harsh derisive comment,
The grackle's laughter; and again we see
His thievish eye, aware amid green boughs.

[13]

Touch earth again: take up your shovel: dig
In the wormy ground. That tree magnificent
Sways like a giant dancer in a garment
Whose gold and green are naught but tricks of
    light.
And at the heart of all that drunken beauty
Is a small lively cynic bird who laughs.

Who sees the vision coming? Who can tell
What moment out of time will be the seed
To root itself, as swift as lightning roots
Into a cloud, and grow, swifter than thought,
And flower gigantic in the infinite?
Walk softly through your forest, and be ready
To hear the horn of horns. Or in your garden
Stoop, but upon your back be ever conscious
Of sunlight, and a shadow that may grow.

KING BORBORIGMI

You say you heard King Borborigmi laugh?
Say how it was.   Some heavenly body moved him?
The moon laughed first?   Dark earth put up a
    finger
Of honeysuckle, through his moonlit window,
And tickled him?

       —King Borborigmi laughed
Alone, walking alone in an empty room,
Thinking, and yet not thinking, seeing, yet blind.
One hand was on his chin, feeling the beard
That razors could not stay; the other groped;
For it was dark, and in the dark were chairs;
Midnight, or almost midnight; Aldebaran
Hanging among the dews.

       —King Borborigmi
Laughed once or twice at nothing, just as midnight
Released a flock of bells?
            —Not this alone;
Not bells in flight toward Aldebaran;

Nor the immitigable beard; nor dews
Heavily pattering on the pent-house roof;
Nor chairs in shadow which his foot disturbed.
Yet it was all of these, and more: the air
Twirling the curtain where a red moth hung:
The one bell flying later than the others
Into the starstrung silence: the garden breaking
To let a thousand seedlings have their way:
An eye-tooth aching, and the pendulum
That heavily ticked upon the leftward swing.

—These trifles woke the laughter of a king?

—Much less than these, and more! He softly
    stepped
Among the webby world, and felt it shudder.
Under the earth—a strand or two of web—
He saw his father's bones, fallen apart,
The jawbone sunken and the skull caved in.
Among his mother's bones a cactus rooted,
And two moles crept, and ants held carnival.
Above the obscene tomb an aloe blossomed; ＼
Dew glistened on the marble. This he saw,
And at the selfsame moment heard the cook
Wind the alarm-clock in her bedroom, yawn,
And creak the bed. And it was then, surprised,

KING BORBORIGMI

He touched a chair, and laughed, and twitched
    the curtain,—
And the moth flew out.

          —Alas, poor Borborigmi,
That it should be so little, and so sorry
A thing to make him laugh!

          —Young Borborigmi,
Saw more than this. The infinite octopus
With eyes of chaos and long arms of stars,
And belly of void and darkness, became clear
About him, and he saw himself embraced
And swept along a vein, with chairs and teeth,
Houses and bones and gardens, cooks and clocks;
The midnight bell, a snoring cook, and he,
Mingled and flowed like atoms.

          —It was this
That made him laugh—to see himself as one
Corpuscle in the infinite octopus? . . .
And was this all, old fool, old turner of
    leaves? . . .

—Alone, thinking alone in an empty room
Where moonlight and the mouse were met
    together,

And pulse and clock together ticked, and dew
Made contrapuntal patter, Borborigmi
Fathomed in his own viscera the world,
Went downward, sounding like a diver, holding
His peakèd nose; and when he came up, laughed.
These things and others saw. But laſt of all,
Ultimate or penultimate, he saw
The one thing that undid him!

        —What was this?
The one grotesquer thing among grotesques?
Carrion, offal, or the toothbrush ready
For carnal fangs? Cancer, that graſps the heart,
Or fungus, whitely swelling in the brain?
Some gargoyle of the thought?

        —King Borborigmi,
Twitching the curtain as the laſt bell flew
Melodious to Aldebaran, beheld
The moth fly also. Downward dropped it softly
Among dropped petals, white. And there one
    rose
Was open in the moonlight! Dew was on it;
The bat, with ragged wing, cavorting, sidling,
Snapped there a sleeping bee—

        —And crunched the moth? . . .

KING BORBORIGMI

—It was the rose in moonlight, crimson, yet
Blanched by the moon; the bee asleep; the bat
And fallen moth—but most the guileless rose.
Guileless! . . . King Borborigmi struck his foot
Against a chair, and saw the guileless rose
Joining himself (King Bubblegut), and all
Those others—the immitigable beard;
Razors and teeth; his mother's bones; the tomb:
The yawning cook; the clock; the dew; the bells
Bursting upward like bubbles—; all so swept
Along one vein of the infinite octopus
With eyes of chaos and long arms of stars
And belly of void and darkness. It was then
He laughed; as he would never laugh again.
For he saw everything; and, in the centre
Of corrupt change, one guileless rose; and laughed
For puzzlement and sorrow.

                              —Ah, poor man,
Poor Borborigmi, young, to be so wise!

—Wise? No. For what he laughed at was just
     this:
That to see all, to know all, is to rot.
So went to bed; and slept; is sleeping still,
If none has waked him.
                    [19]

      —Dead? King Borborigmi
Is dead? Died laughing? Sleeps a dreamless
    sleep
Till cook's alarm clock wakes him?

       —Sleeps like Hamlet,
King of infinite space in a walnut shell—
But has bad dreams; I fear he has bad dreams.

AND IN THE HANGING GARDENS

And in the hanging gardens there is rain
From midnight until one, striking the leaves
And bells of flowers, and stroking boles of planes,
And drawing slow arpeggios over pools,
And stretching strings of sound from eaves to
    ferns.
The princess reads. The knave of diamonds
    sleeps.
The king is drunk, and flings a golden goblet
Down from the turret window (curtained with
    rain)
Into the lilacs.

           And at one o'clock
The vulcan under the garden wakes and beats
The gong upon his anvil. Then the rain
Ceases, but gently ceases, dripping still,
And sound of falling water fills the dark
As leaves grow bold and upright, and as eaves
Part with water. The princess turns the page
Beside the candle, and between two braids
Of golden hair. And reads: "From there I went

Northward a journey of four days, and came
To a wild village in the hills, where none
Was living save the vulture and the rat,
And one old man, who laughed, but could not
    ſpeak.
The roofs were fallen in; the well grown over
With weed; and it was there my father died.
Then eight days further, bearing slightly weſt,
The cold wind blowing sand againſt our faces,
The food taſting of sand.   And as we ſtood
By the dry rock that marks the higheſt point
My brother said: 'Not too late is it yet
To turn, remembering home.'   And we were
    silent
Thinking of home."   The princess shuts her eyes
And feels the tears forming beneath her eyelids
And opens them, and tears fall on the page.
The knave of diamonds in the darkened room
Throws off his covers, sleeps, and snores again.
The king goes slowly down the turret ſtairs
To find the goblet.

             And at two o'clock
The vulcan in his smithy underground
Under the hanging gardens, where the drip
Of rain among the clematis and ivy
Still falls from sipping flower to purple flower,

Smites twice his anvil, and the murmur comes
Among the roots and vines. The princess reads:
"As I am sick, and cannot write you more,
Nor have not long to live, I give this letter
To him, my brother, who will bear it south
And tell you how I died. Ask how it was,
There in the northern desert, where the grass
Was withered, and the horses, all but one,
Perished" . . . The princess drops her golden
    head
Upon the page between her two white arms
And golden braids. The knave of diamonds
    wakes
And at his window in the darkened room
Watches the lilacs tossing, where the king
Seeks for the goblet.

               And at three o'clock
The moon inflames the lilac heads, and thrice
The vulcan, in his root-bound smithy, clangs
His anvil; and the sounds creep softly up
Among the vines and walls. The moon is round,
Round as a shield above the turret top.
The princess blows her candle out, and weeps
In the pale room, where scent of lilac comes,
Weeping, with hands across her eyelids, thinking
Of withered grass, withered by sandy wind.

The knave of diamonds, in his darkened room,
Holds in his hands a key, and softly steps
Along the corridor, and slides the key
Into the door that guards her. Meanwhile,
  slowly,
The king, with raindrops on his beard and hands,
And dripping sleeves, climbs up the turret stairs,
Holding the goblet upright in one hand;
And pauses on the midmost step, to taste
One drop of wine, wherewith wild rain has mixed.

THE WEDDING

At noon, Tithonus, withered by his singing,
Climbing the oatstalk with his hairy legs,
Met grey Arachne, poisoned and shrunk down
By her own beauty; pride had shrivelled both.
In the white web—where seven flies hung
    wrapped—
She heard his footstep; hurried to him; bound
    him;
Enshrouded him in silk; then poisoned him.
Twice shrieked Tithonus, feebly; then was still.
Arachne loved him. Did he love Arachne?
She watched him with red eyes, venomous sparks,
And the furred claws outspread . . . "O sweet
    Tithonus!
Darling! Be kind, and sing that song again!
Shake the bright web again with that deep fiddling!
Are you much poisoned? sleeping? do you dream?
Darling Tithonus!"

          And Tithonus, weakly
Moving one hairy shin against the other
Within the silken sack, contrived to fiddle

A little tune, half-hearted: "Shrewd Arachne!
Whom pride in beauty withered to this shape
As pride in singing shrivelled me to mine—
Unwrap me, let me go—and let me limp,
With what poor strength your venom leaves me, down
This oatstalk, and away."

                Arachne, angry,
Stung him again, twirling him with rough paws,
The red eyes keen. "What! You would dare
    to leave me?
Unkind Tithonus! Sooner I'll kill and eat you
Than let you go. But sing that tune again—
So plaintive was it!"

                And Tithonus faintly
Moved the poor fiddles, which were growing cold,
And sang: "Arachne, goddess envied of gods,
Beauty's eclipse eclipsed by angry beauty,
Have pity, do not ask the withered heart
To sing too long for you! My strength goes out,
Too late we meet for love. O be content
With friendship, which the noon sun once may
    kindle
To give one flash of passion, like a dewdrop,
Before it goes! . . . Be reasonable,—Arachne!"

THE WEDDING

Arachne heard the song grow weaker, dwindle
To first a rustle, and then half a rustle,
And last a tick, so small no ear could hear it
Save hers, a spider's ear. And her small heart,
(Rusted away, like his, to a pinch of dust,)
Gleamed once, like his, and died. She clasped
    him tightly
And sunk her fangs in him. Tithonus dead,
She slept awhile, her last sensation gone;
Woke from the nap, forgetting him; and ate him.

GOD'S ACRE

In Memory Of. In Fondest Recollection Of.
In Loving Memory Of. In Fond
Remembrance. Died in October. Died at Sea.
Who died at sea? The name of the seaport
Escapes her, gone, blown with the eastwind, over
The tombs and yews, into the apple orchard,
Over the road, where gleams a wagon-top,
And gone. The eastwind gallops up from sea
Bringing salt and gulls. The marsh smell, too,
Strong in September; mud and reeds, the reeds
Rattling like bones.

　　　　　She shifts the grass-clipper
From right to left hand, clips and clips the grass.
The broken column, carefully broken, on which
The blackbird hen is laughing—in fondest
　　memory.
Burden! Who was this Burden, to be remem-
　　bered?
Or Potter? The Potter rejected by the Pot.
"Here lies Josephus Burden, who departed
This life the fourth of August, nineteen hundred.

'And He Said Come'." Josephus Burden, forty,
Gross, ribald, with strong hands on which grew
    hair,
And red ears kinked with hair, and northblue eyes,
Held in one hand a hammer, in the other
A nail.   He drove the nail.   .   .   .   This was
    enough?
Or—also—did he love?

                     She changes back
The clipper.   The blades are dull.   The grass is
    wet
And gums the blades.   In Loving Recollection.
Four chains, heavy, hang round the vault.   What
    chance
For skeletons?   The dead men rise at night,
Rattle the links.   "Too heavy! can't be budged . . .
Try once   again — together — NOW! . . . no
    use."
They sit in moonless shadow, gently talking.
"Old Jones it must have been, who made those
    chains.
I'd like to see him lift them now!" . . . The owl
That hunts in Wickham Wood comes over,
    mewing.
"An owl," says one.   "Most likely," says another.
They turn grey heads.

The seawind brings a breaking
Bell sound among the yews and tombstones, ringing
The twisted whorls of bronze on sunlit stones.
Sacred . . . memory . . . affectionate . . .
   O God
What travesty is this—the blackbird soils
The broken column; the worm at work in the
   skull
Feasts on medulla; and the lewd thrush cracks
A snailshell on the vault. He died on shipboard—
Sea-burial, then, were better?

                On her knees
She clips and clips, kneeling against the sod,
Holding the world between her two knees, pon-
   dering
Downward, as if her thought, like men or apples,
Fell ripely into earth. Seablue, her eyes
Turn to the sea. Sea-gulls are scavengers,
Cruel of face, but lovely. By the dykes
The reeds rattle, leaping in eastwind, rattling
Like bones. In Fond Remembrance Of. O God,
That life is what it is, and does not change.
You there in earth, and I above you kneeling.
You dead, and I alive.

She prods a plantain
Of too ambitious root.   That largest yew-tree,
Clutching the hill—

She rises from stiff knees,
Stiffly, and treads the pebble path, that leads
Downward, to sea and town.   The marsh smell comes
Healthy and salt, and fills her nostrils.   Reeds
Dance in the eastwind, rattling; warblers dart
Flashing, from swaying reed to reed, and sing.

THE ROAD

Three then came forward out of darkness, one
An old man bearded, his old eyes red with weeping,
A peasant, with hard hands. "Come now," he
    said,
"And see the road, for which our people die.
Twelve miles of road we've made, a little only,
Westward winding. Of human blood and stone
We build; and in a thousand years will come
Beyond the hills to sea."

               I went with them,
Taking a lantern, which upon their faces
Showed years and grief; and in a time we came
To the wild road which wound among wild hills
Westward; and so along this road we stooped,
Silent, thinking of all the dead men, there
Compounded with sad clay. Slowly we moved:
For they were old and weak, had given all
Their life, to build this twelve poor miles of road,
Muddy, under the rain. And in my hand
Turning the lantern, here or there, I saw
Deep holes of water where the raindrop splashed,

And rainfilled footprints in the grass, and heaps
Of broken ſtone, and ruſted ſpades and picks,
And helves of axes. And the old man ſpoke,
Holding my wriſt: "Three hundred years it took
To build these miles of road: three hundred years;
And human lives unnumbered. But the day
Will come when it is done." Then ſpoke another,
One not so old, but old, whose face was wrinkled:
"And when it comes, our people will all sing
For joy, passing from eaſt to weſt, or weſt
To eaſt, returning, with the light behind them;
All meeting in the road and singing there."
And the third said: "The road will be their life;
A heritage of blood. Grief will be in it,
And beauty out of grief. And I can see
How all the women's faces will be bright.
In that time, laughing, they will remember us.
Blow out your lantern now, for day is coming."

My lantern blown out, in a little while
We climbed in long light up a hill, where climbed
The dwindling road, and ended in a field.
Peasants were working in the field, bowed down
With unrewarded work, and grief, and years
Of pain. And as we passed them, one man fell
Into a furrow that was bright with water
And gave a cry that was half cry half song—

"The road . . . the road . . . the road . . ."
    And all then fell
Upon their knees and sang.

               We four passed on
Over the hill, to westward.   Then I felt
How tears ran down my face, tears without num-
    ber;
And knew that all my life henceforth was weeping,
Weeping, thinking of human grief, and human
Endeavour fruitless in a world of pain.
And when I held my hands up they were old;
I knew my face would not be young again.

DEAD LEAF IN MAY

One skeleton-leaf, white-ribbed, a last year's leaf,
Skipped in a paltry gust, whizzed from the dust,
Leapt the small dusty puddle; and sailing then
Merrily in the sunlight, lodged itself
Between two blossoms in a hawthorn tree.
That was the moment: and the world was
    changed.
With that insane gay skeleton of a leaf
A world of dead worlds flew to hawthorn trees,
Lodged in the green forks, rattled, rattled their
    ribs
(As loudly as a dead leaf's ribs can rattle)
Blithely, among bees and blossoms. I cursed,
I shook my stick, dislodged it. To what end?
Its ribs, and all the ribs of all dead worlds,
Would house them now forever as death should:
Cheek by jowl with May.

That was the moment: and my brain flew open
Like a ripe bursting pod. The seed sprang out,
And I was withered, and had given all.
Ripeness at top means rottenness beneath:

The brain divulging seed, the heart is empty:
The little blood goes through it like quicksilver:
The hand is leather, and the world is lost.

Human, who trudge the road from Here to
    There:
Lock the dry oak-leaf's flimsy skeleton
In auricle or ventricle; sail it
Like a gay ship down red Aorta's flood.
Be the paired blossoms with dead ribs between.
Thirst in the There, that you may drink the Here.

CLIFF MEETING

Met on the westworn cliff, where the short grass
Blew on the sea-rock edge, with crowded sea-pinks
And heather, she and I stood face to face,
Strangers, and stared. What's in a face or eye
That gives its secret, when the moment comes,
For nothing, less than nothing? We but looked,
Looked once, looked hard, looked deep; the sea-
        wind spared
The blue still waters of her soul; far down
I saw the ghost I loved. Did she see also,
In my wan eyes, a depth, and a swimming ghost?
Tranced so at cliff's-edge, stood and stared; then
        laughed;
Then sat together in chilly sunlight, watching
The moving brows of foam come round the
        headland,
And rabbits daring the cliff.

                    Her hand, in grass—
(A sea-pink nodded betwixt thumb and finger)
I touched and lifted: she but smiled. Her arm
I scratched with a tiny fork of heather, drawing

A pair of furrows from elbow down to wrist,
White and sharp; she smiled at first, then frowned.
Her mouth, which said no word and gave no name,
I kissed; and as I kissed it, with eyes open,
I saw the sea-pink (caught twixt thumb and finger)
Plucked up unmercifully.

              The sun went down
Between two waves; and as it went, she rose,
Shaking her dress. To-morrow (so she said)
Here by the cliff's-edge we might meet again.
What's in a face or eye that gives its secret
So lightly, when the moment comes? She saw
Weariness in me, love gone down like the sun,
The fleet ghost gone; and as she saw, she drooped.
Beauty waned out of her; the light drained out
From her deep eyes; pathetic seemed she; I
Discomfited, leering upon her, angry
That I had thought I loved her. So, she went:
Miserable, small, self-pitying, down to darkness.
I watched her go, thinking it strange that she—
Meagre, unlovely—should have captured me.

And on the morrow, when she did not come,
There by the cliff's edge, staked, I found a letter
Mystic, insoluble, with few words written,
Saying—(and it was strange, and like a dream,

For, as I read, the words seemed only marks
Of bird-claws in the sand—) that she was gone
Down to the village, darkness, gone forever;
But left this bird for me, that I might know—
What I should know. And in the short grass lay,
There with the sea-pinks, a blue cormorant,
White eyelids closed, and dying. Her I lifted
Between my hands, and laid against my breast,
Striving to warm her heart. The bird was starved;
The eyes drooped open, and the livid beak
Opened a little; and I gave my hands
To her to eat, having no other food;
Thrusting a finger in the beak, that she
Might eat my flesh and live. But she was dying,
And could not move the purple beak, falling
Against my hand, inert; and then I thought
That, seeking to make her eat, I did but hasten
Her death. For in a moment, then, she died.

Along the cliff I walked, taking the bird,
Holding it in my hands. . . . What had she meant
In leaving this blue cormorant for me?
Was she not coming? Everywhere I looked;
By rock and tree; in coigns of heather; even
Down where the moving brows of foam came in.
Nowhere—nowhere. The sun went west behind

Two waves.   It was the hour of parting.   Would
She come not now for that?

               The darkness gathered.
The sea-pinks lost their colour.   And I walked
Along the cliff's-edge, losing all power of thought,
Taking the cormorant into the dark with me.

CHIAROSCURO: ROSE

HE

Fill your bowl with roses: the bowl, too, have of
    crystal.
Sit at the western window.   Take the sun
Between your hands like a ball of flaming crystal,
Poise it to let it fall, but hold it still,
And meditate on the beauty of your existence;
The beauty of this, that you exist at all.

SHE

The sun goes down,—but without lamentation.
I close my eyes, and the stream of my sensation
In this, at least, grows clear to me:
Beauty is a word that has no meaning.
Beauty is naught to me.

HE

The last blurred raindrops fall from the half-clear
    sky,
Eddying lightly, rose-tinged, in the windless wake
    of the sun.
The swallow ascending against cold walls of cloud

Seems winging upward over huge bleak stairs of
    stone.
The raindrop finds its way to the heart of the
    leaf-bud.
But no word finds its way to the heart of you.

SHE

This also is clear in the stream of my sensation:
That I am content, for the moment . . . Let
    me be.
How light the new grass looks with the rain-dust
    on it!
But heart is a word that has no meaning,
Heart means nothing to me.

HE

To the end of the world I pass and back again
In flights of the mind; yet always find you here,
Remote, pale, unattached . . . O Circe too-clear-
    eyed,
Watching amused your fawning tiger-thoughts,
Your wolves, your grotesque apes—relent, relent!
Be less wary for once: it is the evening.

SHE

But if I close my eyes what howlings greet me!
Do not persuade. Be tranquil. Here is flesh
With all its demons. Take it, sate yourself.
But leave my thoughts to me.

SEA HOLLY

Begotten by the meeting of rock with rock,
The mating of rock and rock, rocks gnashing
   together;
Created so, and yet forgetful, walks
The seaward path, puts up her left hand, shades
Blue eyes, the eyes of rock, to see better
In slanting light the ancient sheep (which kneels
Biting the grass) the while her other hand,
Hooking the wicker handle, turns the basket
Of eggs. The sea is high to-day. The eggs
Are cheaper. The sea is blown from the south-
   west,
Confused, taking up sand and mud in waves,
The waves break, sluggish, in brown foam, the
   wind
Disperses (on the sheep and hawthorn) spray,—
And on her cheeks, the cheeks engendered of rock,
And eyes, the colour of rock. The left hand
Falls from the eyes, and undecided slides
Over the left breast on which muslin lightly
Rests, touching the nipple, and then down
The hollow side, virgin as rock, and bitterly
Caresses the blue hip.

                    It was for this,
This obtuse taking of the seaward path,
This stupid hearing of larks, this hooking
Of wicker, this absent observation of sheep
Kneeling in harsh sea-grass, the cool hand shading
The spray-stung eyes—it was for this the rock
Smote itself. The sea is higher today,
And eggs are cheaper. The eyes of rock take in
The seaward path that winds toward the sea,
The thistle-prodder, old woman under a bonnet,
Forking the thistles, her back against the sea,
Pausing, with hard hands on the handle, peering
With rock eyes from her bonnet.

                    It was for this,
This rock-lipped facing of brown waves, half sand
And half water, this tentative hand that slides
Over the breast of rock, and into the hollow
Soft side of muslin rock, and then fiercely
Almost as rock against the hip of rock—
It was for this in midnight the rocks met,
And dithered together, cracking and smoking.

                    It was for this
Barren beauty, barrenness of rock that aches
On the seaward path, seeing the fruitful sea,

SEA HOLLY

Hearing the lark of rock that sings, smelling
The rock-flower of hawthorn, sweetness of rock—
It was for this, stone pain in the stony heart,
The rock loved and laboured; and all is lost.

PSYCHOMACHIA

I

Tent-caterpillars, as you see, (he said)
Have nested in these cherry-trees, and stripped
All sound of leaves from them. You see their
    webs
Like broken harp-strings, of a fairy kind,
Shine in the moonlight.

             And then I to him:
But is this why, when all the houses sleep,
You meet me here,—to tell me only this,
That caterpillars weave their webs in trees?
This road I know. I have walked many times
These sandy ruts. I know these starveling trees,
Their gestures of stiff agony in winter,
And the sharp conscious pain that gnaws them
    now.
But there is mystery, a message learned,
A word flung down from nowhere, caught by you,
And hither brought for me. How shines that
    word,
From what star comes it? . . . This is what I
    seek.

[46]

And he in answer: Can you hear the blood
Cry out like jangled bells from all these twigs;
Or feel the ghosts of blossom touch your face?
Walk you amid these trees as one who walks
Upon a field where lie the newly slain
And those who darkly die? And hear you crying?
Flesh here is torn from flesh. The tongue's
    plucked out.
What speech then would you have, where speech
    is tongueless,
And nothing, nothing, but a welling up of pain?

I answered: You may say these smitten trees,
Being leafless, have no tongues and cannot speak.
How comforts that my question? . . . You have
    come,
I know, as you come always, with a meaning.
What, then, is in your darkness of hurt trees;
What bird, sequestered in that wilderness
Of inarticulate pain, wrong ill-endured,
And death not understood, but bides his time
To sing a piercing phrase? Why sings he not?
I am familiar, long, with pain and death,
Endure as all do, lift dumb eyes to question
Uncomprehended wounds; I have my forest
Of injured trees, whose bare twigs show the moon
Their shameful floating webs; and I have walked,

As now we walk, to listen there to bells
Of pain, bubbles of blood, and ached to feel
The ghosts of blossom pass.   But is there not
The mystery, the fugitive shape that sings
A sudden beauty there that comes like peace?

You know this road, he said, and how it leads
Beyond starved trees to bare grey poverty grass;
Then lies the marsh beyond, and then the beach,
With dry curled waves of sea-weed, and the sea.
There, in the fog, you hear the row-locks thump,
And there you see the fisherman come in
From insubstantial nothing to a shore
As dim and insubstantial.   He is old,
His boat is old and grey, the oars are worn.
You know this,—you have seen this?

                    And then I:
I know, have seen this, and have felt the shore
As dim and thin as mist; and I have wondered
That it upheld me, did not let me fall
Through nothing into nothing . . . And the oars,
Worn down like human nerves against the world;
And the worn road that leads to sleeping houses
And weeping trees.   But is this all you say?
For there is mystery, a word you have
That shines within your mind.   Now speak that
      word.

And he in answer: So you have the landscape
With all its nerves and voices. It is yours.
Do with it what you will. But never try
To go away from it, for that is death.
Dwell in it, know its houses, and cursed trees,
And call it sorrow. Is this not enough?
Love you not shameful webs? It is enough.
There is no need for bird, or sudden peace.

II

The plain no herbage had, but all was bare
And swollen livid sand in ridges heaped;
And in the sharp cold light that filled the east
Beneath one cloud that was a bird with wings
I saw a figure shape itself, as whirling
It took up sand and moved across the sand.
A man it was, and here and there he ran
Beating his arms, now falling, rising now,
Struggling, for so it seemed, against the air.
But, as I watched, the cloud that was a bird
Lifted its wings; and the white light intense
Poured down upon him. Then I saw him, naked,
Amid that waste, at war with a strange beast
Or monster, many-armed and ever-changing;
That now was like an octopus of air,
Now like a spider with a woman's hair
And woman's hands, and now was like a vine

[49]

That wrapped him round with leaves and sudden
    flowers,
And now was like a huge white thistledown
Floating; and with this changing shape he fought
Furious and exhausted, till at length
I saw him fall upon it in the sand
And strangle it. Its tentacles of leaves
Fell weakly downward from his back, its flowers
Turned black. And then, as he had whirled at
    first,
So whirled he now again, and with his feet
Drew out the sand, and made a pit, and flung
The scorpion-woman-vine therein, and heaped
The sand above.

           And then I heard him sing
And saw him dance; and all that swollen plain
Where no herb grew, became a paradise
Of flowers, and smoking grass, and blowing trees
That shook out birds and song of birds. And he
In power and beauty shining like a demon
Danced there, until that cloud that was a bird
Let fall its wings and darkened him, and hid
The shining fields. But still for long I heard
His voice, and bird-song bells about him chiming,
And knew him dancing there above that grave.

III

Said he: Thus draw your secret sorrow forth,
Whether it wear a woman's face or not;
Walk there at dusk beside that grove of trees,
And sing, and she will come. For while she haunts
Your shameful wood with all its webs and wounds
And darkly broods and works her mischief there,
No peace you'll have, but snares, and poisonous
    flowers
And trees in lamentation. Call her out
As memory cries the white ghost from the tomb.
Play the sharp lyric flute, for that she loves,
With topaz phrases for her vanity.

And I in answer: She is dear to me,
Dearer that in my mind she makes a dark
Of woods and rocks and thorns and venomous
    flowers.
What matter that I seldom see her face,
Or have her beauty never? She is there,
It is her voice I hear in cries of trees.
This may be misery, but it is blest.

Then he: And when you have her, strongly take
Her protean fiery body and lithe arms
And wailing mouth and growing vines of hair
And leaves that turn to hands, and bear her forth

Into that landscape that is rightly yours
And dig a grave for her, and thrust her in
All writhing, and so cover her with earth.
Then will the two, as should be, fuse in one.
The landscape, that was dead, will straightway
    shine
And sing and flower about you, trees will grow
Where desert was, water will flash from dust,
And rocks grow out in leaves. And you, this grief
Torn from your heart and planted in your world,
Will know yourself at peace.

               But will it be,—
I asked,—as bright a joy to see that landscape
Put on diffused her wonder, sing her name,
Burn with the vital secret of her body
There locked in earth like fire, as now to have
Her single beauty fugitive in my mind?
If she is lost, will flowering rocks give peace?

And he in answer: So you have the landscape
With all her nerves and voices . . . She is yours.

ELDER TREE

"The sensual will have its moment? The brain
Sleep? . . . You can prophesy? . . ."

        —Thus laughed the woman,
Tall, thin, and bitter as an elder tree,
Lifting her white face like a crown of bloom.
And so I swore by darkness, trees, and blood,
And rivers underground, and felt my brain,
(Thus challenged by her brain) fall steeply down
Like a dead leaf upon the rushing flood.
"Yes, I can prophesy," I laughed in answer;
And lost my life in hers, which brighter shone,
Radiant and derisive. "Never yet,"
She darkly smiled, "has voice of man flown in
To break my chords of being. You but waste
The evening, with its bank of clouds, where stars
Plunge down to swim . . . Look, how the lights
    now come
Like perforations in that wall of trees—
Wherethrough the Ultimate winks!" . . .

         And she was still,
Clasping long hands around her lifted knee.

These touched I twice, with teasing finger-tip,
Three times and four, then wearied. But the
    darkness
And that profounder sound where rushed the
    river,
Nocturnal, under all, and moving all,—
Took both of us, annulled the brain, devoured
The elder tree, with white faint face of bloom,
And me, who sat beneath it.

                Then my blood
Was filled with elder blossom cold and white,
My arms embraced the tree of singing wood,
My hands took leaves and broke them. We were
    lost,
Thus mingled, in the world. No speech we had.
Till suddenly (as at the end of death,
The darkness being silent) we stood up
Once more; the woman hushed, an elder tree,
And I a voice. And then she smiled, and said—
"Ah, it is true! The sensual has its moment.
The trickster brain—thank God—can be de-
    posed . . ."

Then I, "Look now! how all the trees rush back
From the dark stream! and every blade of grass
New-washed in starlight!"

ELDER TREE

"Starlight?" . . . She laughed, rustling,—
Rustling, nodding her elder-blossom face,—
"Not starlight, no! The trees, the grass, the
    brain,
Come back again from blood; and they are
    strong."

EXILE

These hills are sandy.   Trees are dwarfed here.
    Crows
Caw dismally in skies of an arid brilliance,
Complain in dusty pine-trees.   Yellow daybreak
Lights on the long brown slopes a frost-like dew,
Dew as heavy as rain; the rabbit tracks
Show sharply in it, as they might in snow.
But it's soon gone in the sun—what good does it
    do?
The houses, on the slope, or among brown trees,
Are grey and shrivelled.   And the men who live
    here
Are small and withered, spider-like, with large
    eyes.

Bring water with you if you come to live here—
Cold tinkling cisterns, or else wells so deep
That one looks down to Ganges or Himalayas.
Yes, and bring mountains with you, white, moon-
    bearing,
Mountains of ice.   You will have need of these
Profundities and peaks of wet and cold.

EXILE

Bring also, in a cage of wire or osier,
Birds of a golden colour, who will sing
Of leaves that do not wither, watery fruits
That heavily hang on long melodious boughs
In the blue-silver forests of deep valleys.

I have now been here—how many years? Years
 unnumbered,
My hands grow clawlike. My eyes are large and
 starved.
I brought no bird with me, I have no cistern
Where I might find the moon, or river, or snow.
Some day, for lack of these, I'll spin a web
Between two dusty pine-tree tops, and hang there
Face downward, like a spider, blown as lightly
As ghost of leaf. Crows will caw about me.
Morning and evening I shall drink the dew.

TÉTÉLESTAI

I

How shall we praise the magnificence of the dead,
The great man humbled, the haughty brought to
    dust?
Is there a horn we should not blow as proudly
For the meanest of us all, who creeps his days,
Guarding his heart from blows, to die obscurely?
I am no king, have laid no kingdoms waste,
Taken no princes captive, led no triumphs
Of weeping women through long walls of trum-
    pets;
Say rather, I am no one, or an atom;
Say rather, two great gods, in a vault of starlight,
Play ponderingly at chess, and at the game's end
One of the pieces, shaken, falls to the floor
And runs to the darkest corner; and that piece
Forgotten there, left motionless, is I. . . .
Say that I have no name, no gifts, no power,
Am only one of millions, mostly silent;
One who came with eyes and hands and a heart,
Looked on beauty, and loved it, and then left it.
Say that the fates of time and space obscured me,

TETÉLESTAI

Led me a thousand ways to pain, bemused me,
Wrapped me in ugliness; and like great spiders
Dispatched me at their leisure. . . . Well, what
    then?
Should I not hear, as I lie down in dust,
The horns of glory blowing above my burial?

II

Morning and evening opened and closed above me:
Houses were built above me; trees let fall
Yellowing leaves upon me, hands of ghosts;
Rain has showered its arrows of silver upon me
Seeking my heart; winds have roared and tossed
    me;
Music in long blue waves of sound has borne me
A helpless weed to shores of unthought silence;
Time, above me, within me, crashed its gongs
Of terrible warning, sifting the dust of death;
And here I lie. Blow now your horns of glory
Harshly over my flesh, you trees, you waters!
You stars and suns, Canopus, Deneb, Rigel,
Let me, as I lie down, here in this dust,
Hear, far off, your whispered salutation!
Roar now above my decaying flesh, you winds,
Whirl out your earth-scents over this body, tell me
Of ferns and stagnant pools, wild roses, hillsides!
Anoint me, rain, let crash your silver arrows

On this hard flesh! I am the one who named you,
I lived in you, and now I die in you.
I your son, your daughter, treader of music,
Lie broken, conquered . . . Let me not fall in
　　silence.

III

I, the restless one; the circler of circles;
Herdsman and roper of stars, who could not
　　capture
The secret of self; I who was tyrant to weaklings,
Striker of children; destroyer of women; corrupter
Of innocent dreamers, and laugher at beauty; I,
Too easily brought to tears and weakness by music,
Baffled and broken by love, the helpless beholder
Of the war in my heart of desire with desire, the
　　struggle
Of hatred with love, terror with hunger; I
Who laughed without knowing the cause of my
　　laughter, who grew
Without wishing to grow, a servant to my own
　　body;
Loved without reason the laughter and flesh of a
　　woman,
Enduring such torments to find her! I who at last
Grow weaker, struggle more feebly, relent in my
　　purpose,

TETÉLESTAI

Choose for my triumph an easier end, look back-
    ward
At earlier conquests; or, caught in the web, cry out
In a sudden and empty despair, 'Tetélestai!'
Pity me, now! I, who was arrogant, beg you!
Tell me, as I lie down, that I was courageous.
Blow horns of victory now, as I reel and am
    vanquished.
Shatter the sky with trumpets above my grave.

IV

. . . Look! this flesh how it crumbles to dust
    and is blown!
These bones, how they grind in the granite of
    frost and are nothing!
This skull, how it yawns for a flicker of time in
    the darkness,
Yet laughs not and sees not! It is crushed by a
    hammer of sunlight,
And the hands are destroyed. . . . Press down
    through the leaves of the jasmine,
Dig through the interlaced roots—nevermore will
    you find me;
I was no better than dust, yet you cannot replace
    me. . . .
Take the soft dust in your hand—does it stir:
    does it sing?

[61]

Has it lips and a heart? Does it open its eyes
    to the sun?

Does it run, does it dream, does it burn with a
    secret, or tremble

In terror of death? Or ache with tremendous
    decisions? . . .

Listen! . . . It says: 'I lean by the river. The
    willows

Are yellowed with bud. White clouds roar up
    from the south

And darken the ripples; but they cannot darken
    my heart,

Nor the face like a star in my heart! . . . Rain
    falls on the water

And pelts it, and rings it with silver. The willow
    trees glisten,

The sparrows chirp under the eaves; but the face
    in my heart

Is a secret of music. . . . I wait in the rain and
    am silent.'

Listen again! . . . It says: 'I have worked, I am
    tired,

The pencil dulls in my hand: I see through the
    window

Walls upon walls of windows with faces behind
    them,

Smoke floating up to the sky, an ascension of
    sea-gulls.

I am tired. I have struggled in vain, my decision
    was fruitless,

Why then do I wait? with darkness, so easy, at
    hand! . . .

But tomorrow, perhaps . . . I will wait and en-
    dure till tomorrow!' . . .

Or again: 'It is dark. The decision is made. I
    am vanquished

By terror of life. The walls mount slowly about
    me

In coldness. I had not the courage. I was for-
    saken.

I cried out, was answered by silence . . . Teté-
    lestai! . . .'

v

Hear how it babbles!—Blow the dust out of your
    hand,

With its voices and visions, tread on it, forget it,
    turn homeward

With dreams in your brain. . . . This, then, is
    the humble, the nameless,—

The lover, the husband and father, the struggler
    with shadows,

The one who went down under shoutings of chaos,
   the weakling
Who cried his 'forsaken!' like Christ on the
   darkening hilltop! . . .
This, then, is the one who implores, as he dwindles
   to silence,
A fanfare of glory. . . . And which of us dares
   to deny him?

THE ROOM

Through that window—all else being extinct
Except itself and me—I saw the struggle
Of darkness against darkness. Within the room
It turned and turned, dived downward. Then I
    saw
How order might—if chaos wished—become:
And saw the darkness crush upon itself,
Contracting powerfully; it was as if
It killed itself: slowly: and with much pain.
Pain. The scene was pain, and nothing but pain.
What else, when chaos draws all forces inward
To shape a single leaf? . . .

               For the leaf came
Alone and shining in the empty room;
After a while the twig shot downward from it;
And from the twig a bough; and then the trunk,
Massive and coarse; and last the one black root.
The black root cracked the walls. Boughs burst
    the window:
The great tree took possession.

Tree of trees!
Remember (when time comes) how chaos died
To shape the shining leaf. Then turn, have
  courage,
Wrap arms and roots together, be convulsed
With grief, and bring back chaos out of shape.
I will be watching then as I watch now.
I will praise darkness now, but then the leaf.

POVERTY GRASS

First, blow the trumpets: call the people hither!
Not merely in the township! Send them further.
Set hornsmen at all crossroads: send out horsemen
With horns, a man's length, bound in brass,
Far to the north, the west. Bid them to blow
Unceasing summons, shatter the air, shake leaves
From trees decrepit. I would have the world
Sound with a bugle music from end to end.
Lead then the people hither, have the roads
Black with the mass of them at night and noon.
And when you have them, see them banked about
    me,
Row behind row — (how shine already the
    faces!) —
Like angels in Angelico's vision of heaven.
Those that were horsemen first will now be
    ushers—
'Stand there!' they'll cry, 'no crowding!—
    Those behind
Will hear, feel, understand, as well as those
Who rest their chins upon him, prop their elbows
Against the coffin-lid! Stand still! be patient!'

As for the house—that must be fit as well.
Thus, as it now stands—no! it is too meagre.
The stage is bare. First, the approach is bad.
The hill, behind, that for a thousand years
Has washed its loam and leaves against these
    walls,—
The hill must go. So, let a thousand axes
Flash against bark: let fall a thousand oaks
With all their crying birds, small scolding
    squirrels,
Bees' nests and birds' nests, hornets, wasps, and
    snakes.
A thousand carts, then, each with a quaking tree
Outstretched in ignominy, chained and helpless,—
These, going hence, will be our first procession:
We'll bear to the sea our captives. Next, an army
With spades and picks a thousand, have them led
To music, up the hill, and then like ants
Devour him: gash him first, and swarm in the
    gash,
Eat inward till he's maggoty with men,—
A hollow seething shell,—and lastly, nothing.
As for the house, its walls must be of glass.
And no partitions! one vast room that's walled
And roofed with clearest crystal. There at night
We'll have great light, ten thousand flames of
    candles,

Ten thousand clear-eyed flames in a crystal casket:
The folk on the utmost hill will see, and cry
'Look, how the moon's caught in a crystal coffin!'
And last, myself, there in that crystal coffin,
Flooded with light, reclining half, half sitting
Propped up amid soft silks in a little box
Of brilliant glass, yet lidless. There I'll sit
Like prophet at a tomb's edge, open-mouthed,
Pale, old, obscene, white-bearded—see! my beard
Hangs on the coffin as a snow-drift hangs
On a wall of ice . . . And there, at last, I'll
    speak.

So, then! You see it clearly. It is night-time.
The house is bright. And I,—in an open coffin
Of glass, that's in the house, a larger coffin,—
(That, too, in the coffin that we call the world,
Large, airy, lucent, lighted with lights of stars,—)
Peer from the luminous grave's-edge into darkness
That's filled from hub to marge with staring
    faces.
Beautiful! Is the world here? Let it gaze, then,
And fill its idiot eyes to overflowing
With a sight not known before. Step closer,
    kings,—
Emperors, use your elbows as the plebs do.
Steam, if you like, with your ambitious breath

These walls that tell no lies. I'd have you hear
    me,
You most of all; though I forget not either
The vast grey hungry maggot-mass of men:
The little wedge-shaped darlings, in their broth
Of carrion illusions! . . . How they rot
The air they breathe, turn the green earth to
    poison,
People the sky with pestilence of sick fancies!
See how the whole sky swarms with dirty
    wings! . . .

O Man, who so corrupt all things you feed on;
Whose meditation slimes the thing it thinks;
Vile borer into the core of the universe;
Spoiler and destroyer; you, ambitious,
Crawling upon your admirable belly
For nothing but that at last your tube-shaped
    mouth
Should blindly thrust and suck at the innermost
    heart
Of the world, or god, or infinite overthrown;
Foulest and most dishonest of all creatures;
Sole traitorous worm of all things living, you
Who crown your horrible head with a dream of
    glory
And call yourself a king! Come closer, hear me,

POVERTY GRASS

I am the prophet who, as through these walls
Of innocent glass, see all things deep and clear,
The after and before, revealed or hid:
Partly among you living, partly dead,
I see your hungry mouths, but also see
With my dead eye,—(one cold eye underground
Beneath the earth's black coffin-lid,—) the dead.
Ha! You would have my secret? You would hear
The one bright shattering trumpet whose long blast
Blows like a whirlwind myriad ghosts from tombs?
You cry to the prophet, do you, for a vision—
You'd have me, with one sombre word of magic,
Cry beauty back from dust, and set to singing
This catacomb of graves you call a world?
Press closer, kings! Swarm over me, you plebs!
Feed your rapacious eyes on me, devour
With mouths and nerves and nostrils and raw
    brains
This bloodless carcase that contains your secret:
Have out my heart, hold up above it candles,
Pass it among you, squeak and growl and jabber,
Stamp it beneath your feet—it's an old leaf
Will turn to a little dust . . . For there's the
    wonder!
I am but poverty grass; a dry grey weed;
A trifling dusty moss, fine-branched as coral—;
One footstep makes it powder. And my secret,—

Which all my horsemen brought you here to
    learn,—
Is nought but this: this singing world of yours
Is but a heap of bones. Sound once the trumpet
And you shall see them, tier upon tier, profound
As God himself! Sound twice the trumpet, then,
And I shall add my bone or two. And after,
At the third blast, will all these lights puff out,—
And you may grope in the darkness, as you came.
Sound the bright horn. Shut, coffin! I am dead.

SOUND OF BREAKING

Why do you cry out, why do I like to hear you
Cry out, here in the dewless evening, sitting
Close, close together, so close that the heart stops
    beating
And the brain its thought? Wordless, worthless
    mortals
Stumbling, exhausted, in this wilderness
Of our conjoint destruction! Hear the grass
Raging about us! Hear the worms applaud!
Hear how the ripples make a sound of chaos!
Hear now, in these and the other sounds of
    evening,
The first brute step of God!

                About your elbow,
Making a ring of thumb and finger, I
Slide the walled blood against the less-walled
    blood,
Move down your arm, surmount the wrist-bone,
    shut
Your long slim hand in mine. Each finger-tip
Is then saluted by a finger-tip;
The hands meet back to back, then face to face;

Then lock together. And we, with eyes averted,
Smile at the evening sky of alabaster,
See nothing, lose our souls in the maelstrom,
    turning
Downward in rapid circles.

                        Bitter woman,
Bitter of heart and brain and blood, bitter as I
Who drink your bitterness—can this be beauty?
Do you cry out because the beauty is cruel?
Terror, because we downward sweep so swiftly?
Terror of darkness?

                It is a sound of breaking,
The world is breaking, the world is a sound of
    breaking,
Many-harmonied, diverse, profound,
A shattering beauty. See, how together we break,
Hear what a crashing of disordered chords and
    discords
Fills the world with falling, when we thus lean
Our two mad bodies together!

                        It is a sound
Of everlasting grief, the sound of weeping,
The sound of disaster and misery, the sound
Of passionate heartbreak at the centre of the
    world.

AN OLD MAN, WEEPING

How can she say this misery? A hand
Of gold, with fingers of brass, plucking
At random, murderously and harshly, among
The stretched strings of the soul? A hand cruel
Yet loved? Deep in the soul it plunges
Twanging and snapping; murderous graceful hand
On which she fawns and weeps.

                            And yet not this
Nor nothing like this. It is a burning tree
Grotesque of shape, yet many-leaved, where-
        through
The wind makes melody.

                            Nor yet this,
It is a music powerful and visible
Shaped like an octopus, each arm a beak
Each beak a murder.

                    Nor yet this, but love
Taloned, with red on talons, and redder mouth,
Singing and striking.

[75]

PRIAPUS AND THE POOL

You, through whom love comes,
Hideous, gaunt, large-boned, arid of face,
Ravaged by sorrow—say why it is that love
Flies to you as the bat flies to its cavern!
Hated woman of wormwood, body steeped
In Lethe, tasting of death!

The carven priest
Gilded and small, with one gilt hand uplifted
And gilded forehead smooth, and coronet
Gilded, and the black eyelashes lowered
To hide the eyes, and passive suffering mouth,
Woodenly murmurs: Tao, the way, the way,
The region Way!

And the red crusted bowl
Shaped by the fleeing potter, eyes intent
On dragons, cries—Give form to formless, shape
The flying chaos!

And last the imprisoned blood,
Pouring darkly from cell to cell of the heart,
Upseethes: Go near her, break her walls down, pour
Blood into blood, embed your brain in hers,

AN OLD MAN, WEEPING

Root your gross thought in her no-less-gross
    thought!
Music with music mingles, be you music
Mingled, let the dissonance, clashed and dissolved,
Pierce with reality the too-smooth song!

(. . . Thus looked she at me on a summer
    evening
With cornflower eyes, sad brow, and aging mouth,
And smiled askance, miserable, dumb, ashamed,
And moved the pathetic bones toward me sadly,
And locked me in her heart, as one might lock
An old man, weeping, in a rusted cage.)

SEVEN TWILIGHTS

I

The ragged pilgrim, on the road to nowhere,
Waits at the granite milestone.   It grows dark.
Willows lean by the water.   Pleas of water
Cry through the trees.   And on the boles and
    boughs
Green water-lights make rings, already paling.
Leaves speak everywhere.   The willow leaves
Silverly stir on the breath of moving water,
Birch-leaves, beyond them, twinkle, and there on
    the hill,
And the hills beyond again, and the highest hill,
Serrated pines, in the dusk, grow almost black.
By the eighth milestone on the road to nowhere
He drops his sack and lights once more the pipe
There often lighted.   In the dusk-sharpened sky
A pair of night-hawks windily sweep, or fall,
Booming, toward the trees.   Thus had it been
Last year, and the year before, and many years:
Ever the same. . . . "Thus turns the human
    track

Backward upon itself, I stand once more
By this small stream. . . ." Now the rich sound
    of leaves,
Turning in air to sway their heavy boughs,
Burns in his heart, sings in his veins, as spring
Flowers in veins of trees; bringing such peace
As comes to seamen when they dream of seas.
"O trees! exquisite dancers in grey twilight!
Witches! fairies! elves! who wait for the moon
To thrust her golden horn, like a golden snail,
Above that mountain!—arch your green benedic-
    tion
Once more over my heart. Muffle the sound of
    bells,
Mournfully human, that cries from the darken-
    ing valley;
Close, with your leaves, about the sound of
    water;
Take me among your hearts as you take the mist
Among your boughs!" . . . Now by the granite
    milestone,
On the ancient human road that leads to no-
    where,
The pilgrim listens, as the night air brings
The murmured echo, perpetual, from the gorge
Of barren rock far down the valley. Now,
Though twilight here, it may be starlight there;

Mist makes elfin lakes in the hollow fields;
The dark wood stands in the mist like a sombre
    island
With one red star above it. . . . "This I should
    see,
Should I go on, follow the falling road,—
This I have often seen. . . . But I shall stay
Here, where the ancient milestone, like a watch-
    man,
Lifts up its figure eight, its one grey knowledge,
Into the twilight; as a watchman lifts
A lantern, which he does not know is out."

II

Now by the wall of the little town I lean
Myself, like ancient wall and dust and sky,
And the purple dusk, grown old, grown old in
    heart.
Shadows of clouds flow inward from the sea.
The mottled fields grow dark. The golden wall
Grows grey again, turns stone again; the tower,
No longer kindled, darkens against a cloud.
Old is the world, old as the world am I;
The cries of sheep rise upward from the fields,
Forlorn and strange; and wake an ancient echo
In fields my blood has known, but has not seen.

"These fields"—(an unknown voice beyond the
    wall
Murmurs)—"were once the province of the sea.
Where now the sheep graze, mermaids were at
    play;
Sea-horses galloped; and the great jewelled tor-
    toise
Walked slowly, looking upward at the waves,
Bearing upon his back a thousand barnacles,
A white acropolis. . . ." The ancient tower
Sends out, above the houses and the trees,
And the flat fields below the mouldered walls,
A measured phrase of bells. And in the silence
I hear a woman's voice make answer then:
"Well, they are green, although no ship can sail
    them.
Sky-larks rest in the grass, and start up singing
Before the girl who stoops to pick sea-poppies.
Spiny, the poppies are, and oh how yellow!
And the brown clay is runnelled by the rain."
A moment since, the sheep that crop the grass
Had long blue shadows, and the grass-tips
    sparkled:
Now all grows old. . . . O voices strangely
    speaking,
Voices of man and woman, voices of bells,
Diversely making comment on our time

Which flows and bears us with it into dark,—
Repeat the things you say! Repeat them slowly
Upon this air, make them an incantation
For ancient tower, old wall, the purple twilight,
This dust, and me! . . . But all I hear is si-
    lence,
And something that may be leaves or may be sea.

III

When the tree bares, the music of it changes:
Hard and keen is the sound, long and mournful;
Pale are the poplar boughs in the evening light
Above my house, against a slate-cold cloud.
When the house ages, and the tenants leave it,
Cricket sings in the tall grass by the threshold;
Spider, by the cold mantel, hangs his web.
Here, in a hundred years from that clear season
When first I came here bearing lights and music,
To this old ghostly house my ghost will come,—
Pause in the half-light, turn by the poplar, glide
Above tall grasses through the broken door.
Who will say that he saw—or the dusk deceived
    him—
A mist with hands of mist blow down from the
    tree
And open the door and enter and close it after?
Who will say that he saw, as midnight struck

Its tremulous golden twelve, a light in the win-
    dow,
And first heard music, as of an old piano,
Music remote, as if it came from the earth,
Far down; and then, in the quiet, eager voices?
" . . . Houses grow old and die, houses have
    ghosts—
Once in a hundred years we return, old house,
And live once more." . . . And then the ancient
    answer,
In a voice not human, but more like creak of
    boards
Or rattle of panes in the wind—"Not as the
    owner,
But as a guest you come, to fires not lit
By hands of yours. . . . Through these long-si-
    lent chambers
Move slowly, turn, return, and bring once more
Your lights and music. It will be good to talk."

IV

"This is the hour," she said, "of transmutation:
It is the eucharist of the evening, changing
All things to beauty. Now the ancient river,
That all day under the arch was polished jade,
Becomes the ghost of a river, thinly gleaming

[83]

Under a silver cloud.   It is not water:
It is that azure stream in which the stars
Bathe at the daybreak and become immortal."
"And the moon," said I—not thus to be outdone—
"What of the moon?   Over the dusty plane-
    trees,
Which crouch in the dusk above their feeble lan-
    terns,
Each coldly lighted by his tiny faith;
The moon, the waxen moon, now almost full,
Creeps whitely up. . . . Westward the waves of
    cloud,
Vermilion, crimson, violet, stream on the air,
Shatter to golden flakes in the icy green
Translucency of twilight.   And the moon
Drinks up their light, and as they fade or darken,
Brightens.   O monstrous miracle of the twilight,
That one should live because the others die!"
"Strange too," she answered, "that upon this
    azure
Pale-gleaming ghostly stream, impalpable—
So faint, so fine that scarcely it bears up
The petals that the lantern strews upon it,—
These great black barges float like apparitions,
Loom in the silver of it, beat upon it,
Moving upon it as dragons move on air!"

"Thus always," then I answered,—looking never
Toward her face, so beautiful and strange
It grew, with feeding on the evening light,—
"The gross is given by inscrutable God
Power to beat wide wings upon the subtle.
Thus we ourselves, so fleshly, fallible, mortal,
Stand here, for all our foolishness, transfigured:
Hung over nothing in an arch of light;
While one more evening, like a wave of silence,
Gathers the stars together and goes out."

v

Now the great wheel of darkness and low clouds
Whirs and whirls in heaven with dipping rim;
Against the ice-white wall of light in the west
Skeleton trees bow down in a stream of air.
Leaves, black leaves and smoke, are blown on the
    wind;
Mount upward past my window; swoop again;
In a sharp silence, loudly, loudly falls
The first cold drop, striking a shrivelled leaf.
Doom and dusk for the earth! Upward I reach
To draw chill curtains and shut out the dark,
Pausing an instant, with uplifted hand,
To watch, between black ruined portals of cloud,

One star,—the tottering portals fall and crush it.
Here are a thousand books! here is the wisdom
Alembicked out of dust, or out of nothing;
Choose now the weightiest word, most golden
    page,
Most sombrely musicked line; hold up these lan-
    terns,—
These paltry lanterns, wisdoms, philosophies,—
Above your eyes, against this wall of darkness;
And you'll see—what? One hanging strand of
    cobweb;
A window-sill a half-inch deep in dust.
Speak out, old wise-men! Now, if ever, we need
    you.
Cry loudly, lift shrill voices like magicians
Against this baleful dusk, this wail of rain!
But you are nothing. Your pages turn to water
Under my fingers: cold, cold and gleaming,
Arrowy in the darkness, rippling, dripping—
All things are rain. Myself, this lighted room,
What are we but a murmurous pool of rain?
The slow arpeggios of it, liquid, sibilant,
Thrill and thrill in the dark. World-deep I lie
Under a sky of rain. Thus lies the sea-shell
Under the rustling twilight of the sea;

No gods remember it; no understanding
Cleaves the long darkness with a sword of light.

VI

Heaven, you say, will be a field in April,
A friendly field, a long green wave of earth,
With one domed cloud above it.   There you'll lie
In noon's delight, with bees to flash above you,
Drown amid buttercups that blaze in the wind,
Forgetting all save beauty.   There you'll see
With sun-filled eyes your one great dome of cloud
Adding fantastic towers and spires of light,
Ascending, like a ghost, to melt in the blue.
Heaven enough, in truth, if you were there!
Could I be with you, I would choose your noon,
Drown amid buttercups, laugh with the intimate
        grass,
Dream there forever. . . . But, being older,
        sadder,
Having not you, nor aught save thought of you,
It is not spring I'll choose, but fading summer;
Not noon I'll choose, but the charmed hour of
        dusk.
Poppies?   A few!   And a moon almost as red.
But most I'll choose that subtler dusk that comes
Into the mind—into the heart, you say—
When, as we look bewildered at lovely things,

Striving to give their loveliness a name,
They are forgotten; and other things, remembered,
Flower in the heart with the fragrance we call
grief.

VII

In the long silence of the sea, the seaman
Strikes twice his bell of bronze. The short note
wavers
And loses itself in the blue realm of water.
One sea-gull, paired with a shadow, wheels,
wheels;
Circles the lonely ship by wave and trough;
Lets down his feet, strikes at the breaking water,
Draws up his golden feet, beats wings, and rises
Over the mast. Light from a crimson cloud
Crimsons the sluggishly creeping foams of waves;
The seaman, poised in the bow, rises, falls,
As the deep forefoot finds a way through waves;
And there below him, steadily gazing westward,—
Facing the wind, the sunset, the long cloud,—
The goddess of the ship, proud figurehead,
Smiles inscrutably, plunges to crying waters,
Emerges streaming, gleaming, with jewels falling
Fierily from carved wings and golden breasts;
Steadily glides a moment, then swoops again.

Carved by the hand of man, grieved by the wind;
Worn by the tumult of all the tragic seas,
Yet smiling still, unchanging, smiling still
Inscrutably, with calm eyes and golden brow—
What is it that she sees and follows always,
Beyond the molten and ruined west, beyond
The light-rimmed sea, the sky itself? What
    secret
Gives wisdom to her purpose? Now the cloud
In final conflagration pales and crumbles
Into the darkening water. Now the stars
Burn softly through the dusk. The seaman strikes
His small lost bell again, watching the west
As she below him watches. . . . O pale goddess,
Whom not the darkness, even, or rain or storm,
Changes; whose great wings are bright with foam,
Whose breasts are cold as the sea, whose eyes
    forever
Inscrutably take that light whereon they look—
Speak to us! Make us certain, as you are,
That somewhere, beyond wave and wave and
    wave,
That dreamed-of harbour lies which we would
    find.

ELECTRA

I

The little princess, on her eleventh birthday,
Trapped a blue butterfly in a net of gauze,
Where it was sunning on a speckled stone.
The blue wings fluttered in the silkworm net.
"What voice, Blue Butterfly," (the Princess cried)
"Is voice of butterfly? . . . You scream in fury
Close to my ear; yet hear I not a sound."
She caught it down against the stone, and pressed
A royal finger on each round blue wing;
And as one tears apart a folded leaf
By pushing right and left, so tore she, smiling,
The azure fly. . . . Her eyes were bright and
  blue,
Her teeth were sharp; the sunlight streaked her
  hair
With twining gold along two braids. She frowned
As might a chemist at a test-tube-drop
(Bright, poisonous and pendent) when she saw
Cerulean dust upon each finger tip.
This, being rubbed against a tulip-mouth,
(A glutted bee dislodged) she sat demurely:
Opened her book, on which leaf-shadows winked;

And blew a dart toward a scarlet bird
In bright green tropics of the Amazon.

II

Dressing the naked doll of redded wax,
(The white cheeks rouged) she feather-stitched
    a square
Of scarlet silk with golden staggering stitches;
Chain-lightninged all its edges. After this,
A square of azure silk, a square of purple,
Superimposed; and then a tinfoil crown,
Massive, of divers colours; this, compounded
(Relics of Beaune, of Jerez, and Oporto)
Blazed the wax brow. A bed of cottonwool
Was smoothed; and thrice-anointed Ferdinand
(First pressed against her thigh for nourish-
    ment)
Was covered with a soiled green handkerchief
And closed his eyes: exchanging glass for wax.

This was the seventh year. Between the eighth
And ninth, the form of nourishment was changed.
The doll was clasped between her knees. She
    held
A knife in one hand, while the other lifted
A paper bird. The neck of this was severed.
And Ferdinand had passed from milk to blood.

[91]

III

"Your soul" (so said her father in the spring
That brought her sixteenth year) "turns smaller,
    as
Your body waxes to ripe beauty. Dwarfs
(As you have seen in circuses, or tumbling
Through scarlet-papered hoops, at vaudeville)
Bear on the brow, though mouth and eyes be fair,
A drawn and arid look, of suffering.
Dwarfed, and as blue and arid, peers the soul
Like a starved nymph from your bright eyes.
    Your mouth
Though beautiful, and, yes, desirable,—
(Even to me, who like a wizard shaped it),—
Is much too red; too cruelly downward curved,
It hides a tooth too sharp. You will do murder—
Laughing and weeping; hear the song of blood;
The gnome in you will laugh; the nymph will
    weep."

She locked strong hands around his neck and
    kissed him.
Lifting a naked knee to press him subtly
She hurt him consciously; kissed till he laughed;
Unlocked her hands, then, sobered; moved away;
Shook down the golden skirt; whistled a tune;
And read the morning paper, coiled like a cat.

IV

"Under this water-lily knee" (she said)
"Blood intricately flows, corpuscle creeps,
The white like sliced cucumber, and the red
Like poker-chip. Along dark mains they flow
As wafts the sponging heart. The water-lily,
Subtle in seeming, bland to lover's hand
Upthrust exploring, is in essence gross,
Multiple and corrupt. Thus, in the moonlight"
(She hooked a curtain and disclosed the moon)
"How cold and lucent! And this naked breast,
Whereon a blue vein writes Diana's secret,
How simple! How seductive of the palm
That flatters with the finest tact of flesh!
Not silver is this flank, nor ivory,
Gold it is not, not copper, but distilled
Of lust in moonlight, and my own hand strays
To touch it in this moonlight, whence it came."
Naked in moonlight, like a doll of wax,
On the stone floor nocturnal, she stood still
But moved her hands. The cruel mouth was
    curved,
Smiling a little; and her eyes were fixed,
In wonder, on Diana's hieroglyph.
And it was then (her nineteenth autumn come)
She heard at last, so often prophesied,
The singing of the blood. Her beauty broke

To sound beneath her hands, which moved from
    breast
To knee and back again, and bruised the flank
That was not gold or copper, but became
A throbbing sound beneath palpating palms.
Thus stood awhile; then sighed; then dropped
    her hands
And wept, as he (who loved her) had foretold.

V

It was the twentieth birthday, or the moon,
Which flung a careless net upon the house
Trapping the stone (as she had trapped the
    fly);
These, or the emptied heart of night, which filled
The house with weeping. In the room they lay
Weeping together. "Like a harp it is"
(She said) "which but to sound, but once to
    sound,
Snaps every string. Better to die, than be
Conjointly now, henceforth, a broken thing
Where sound of life was once." She pressed his
    hand
Against her side, where once the doll was pressed,
Prince Ferdinand; but she was hungry still.
So then she held him hard between her knees
And heard the song of blood, outrageously,

[94]

And cried, "Shut eyes and kiss me!" "O,
    Arachne!
What web is this you weave, dear poison-mouth?"
"The web, alas, is cut as soon as woven,"
She answered. And the word she ſpoke was
    true.

VI

The moonlight and the house then sang together,
Yet not the house, but something in the house,
As if together they once more diſtilled,
(Of blood and moonlight) ivory or gold,
Copper or silver; or, if not quite these
Something of which the moon contrived the sur-
    face
While blood beneath supplied the essence gross.
Useless! for it was ſpilled as soon as brimmed.
Prince Ferdinand was dead, Arachne dead,
The blood unmoving, and the moonlight vain.

PRIAPUS AND THE POOL

PRIAPUS AND THE POOL

. . . Was God, then, so derisive as to shape us
In the image of Priapus? . . .
(Priapus?   Who was he?)
Are we never to be left by our desires,
But forever try to warm our foolish hearts
At these illusory fires?
(Priapus! . . . do you mean a terminal figure
In a garden by a sea?)
It is strange! for one so easily conceives
A quieter world, in which the flesh and dust
Are contented, do not hunger, or thirst, or
     lust. . . .

(Priapus! . . . But, I don't know who you
     mean.
Do you intimate God played some trick upon
     us? . . .
I will tell you about a pool that I have seen!

It is very old, it is very deep and clear,
No one knows how deep it is,

PRIAPUS AND THE POOL

The ancient trees are about it in an ancient forest,
It is a pool of mysteries!)

. . . It is puzzling, none the less, to understand
How God, if he is less or more than flesh,
Could have devised for us, walking in his garden,
The delicate imperfections of this mesh. . . .

(When it is clear, the pool reflects the trees—
Look down, and you will see the flight of a bird
Among the wavering boughs! But when a breeze
Comes slowly from that wood, the pool is stirred,
And a shadow like the skeleton of a cloud
Shivers like a ghost across it, puffs and
        passes. . . .
When it is still, the sky comes back again,
And at the fringes it reflects the grasses.)

. . . Must we always, like Priapus in a wood,
In the underbrush of our perplexities,
Pursue our maidens—pursuer and pursued? . . .

(I will not say it is not sometimes troubled!
It is very old; strange things are imaged there.
Out of its depths at night the stars have bubbled;
And into its depths maidens have hung their hair.
Leaves have fallen into it without number

And never been found again.
Birds have sung above it in the ancient trees.
And sometimes raindrops fall upon it, and then
There are rings of silver upon it, spreading and
     fading,
Delicately intersecting. . . .
But if you return again when the sky is cloudless,
You will find it clear again, and coldly reflecting.
Reflecting the ancient trees of the ancient forest,
And the ancient leaves, ready to fall once more,
And the blue sky under the leaves, old and empty,
And the savage grasses along the shore.)

. . . Priapus, himself, was never disen-
     chanted. . . .
Why, then, did God permit us to be haunted
By this sense of imperfections? . . .

(But can a pool remember its reflections?
That is the thing that troubles me!
Does it remember the cloud that falls upon it,
Or the indignation of a tree?
Or suppose that once the image of Priapus
Fell quivering in ferocious sunshine there
As he came suddenly upon it from his forest
With fir-cones in his hair—
Would the pool, through the silences thereafter,

Recall that visitation and be stirred
Any more than it would hear and heed the
    laughter
Of a swinging ape, or the singing of a bird?)

. . . Was God, then, so derisive as to shape us
In the image of Priapus? . . .

(It is very old, it is very deep and clear,
No one knows how deep it is!
The ancient trees are about it in an ancient
    forest,
It is a pool of mysteries.)

I

The viola ceased its resonant throbbing, the violin
Was silent, the flute was still.
The voice of the singer was suddenly hushed.
    Only
The silence seemed to thrill

With the last echo of music, hovering over
The nodding heads of the listeners bowed and
    few;
And I became aware of the long light through a
    window,
Of the beauty of silence, of the beauty of you

Never so sharply known as when, beside you,
I dared not look to see
What thought shone out of your face, or if, like
    marble,
It hid its thought from me.

Never so lovely had music seemed, as when
Its lips were closed, its beauty said,
Its arrow of sound lost forever in the singing of
    the infinite;
And I could not turn my head,

In the motionless azure of silence that descended
    upon us,
Lest, somehow, you should not be there,
Or shine too much or little with the momentary
    beauty
Of which I was bitterly aware.

It was as if the mingled clear voices of the music,
Which the heart for a moment happily knew,
Had somehow, in the instant of their cessation,
Falling from air, become the beauty of you.

O white-flamed chord of many notes miraculously
    sung
In the blue universe of silence there for me:
I shall remember you thus when you are old and
    I am saddened;
And continents darken between us, or the silence
    of the sea.

II

In the moonlight I cry out, in the sunlight I bit-
    terly exclaim,
I curse myself, turning my eyes upon my wretched-
    ness;
Lamentable it is to be caught once more in the
    net of red flame;
Only in the darkness without stars I at last lie
    still.

I have despised the universe that could so scheme
    to capture
The ridiculous sparrow in its futile red net of
    desire.
Now I despise no more. The city shines sud-
    denly with rapture.
The sky burns bright, the trees bend their heads
    in a dream.

Voices of delight rise out of the stones beneath
    my feet,
Azure the dusk is, the waters are singing. Won-
    dering I stand
While the universe deepens about me. Sword-
    sharp-sweet,
Your voice, that I remember faintly, pierces my
    heart.

O light of the clear blue sky, for the first time
    known:
I am the solitary leaf that burns and falls
Shrivelled under your immensity, ecstatically
    blown
Down to the dust and darkness. Forget not me.

III

When trout swim down Great Ormond Street
And sea-gulls cry above them lightly

And hawthorns heave cold flagstones up
To blossom whitely

Against old walls of houses there,
Gustily shaking out in moonlight
Their country sweetness on sweet air;
And in the sunlight

By the green margin of that water
Children dip white feet and shout,
Casting nets in the braided water
To catch the trout:

Then I shall hold my breath and die,
Swearing I never loved you; no,
'You were not lovely!' I shall cry,
'I never loved you so.'

IV

This is the shape of the leaf, and this of the
    flower,
And this the pale bole of the tree
Which watches its bough in a pool of unwaver-
    ing water
In a land we never shall see.

The thrush on the bough is silent, the dew falls
    softly,
In the evening is hardly a sound.

And the three beautiful pilgrims who come here
    together
Touch lightly the dust of the ground,

Touch it with feet that trouble the dust but as
    wings do,
Come shyly together, are still,
Like dancers who wait, in a pause of the music,
    for music
The exquisite silence to fill.

This is the thought of the first, and this of the second,
And this the grave thought of the third:
'Linger we thus for a moment, palely expectant,
And silence will end, and the bird

'Sing the pure phrase, sweet phrase, clear phrase
    in the twilight
To fill the blue bell of the world;
And we, who on music so leaflike have drifted
    together,
Leaflike apart shall be whirled

'Into what but the beauty of silence, silence for-
    ever?' . . .
. . . This is the shape of the tree,
And the flower, and the leaf, and the three pale
    beautiful pilgrims;
This is what you are to me.

V

And already the minutes, the hours, the days,
Separate thoughts and separate ways,
Fall whitely and silently and slowly between us,
Fall between us like phantasmal rain and snow.
And we, who were thrust for an instant so sharply
 together,
Under changing skies to alien destinies go.

Melody heard in the midnight on the wind,—
Orange poppy of fire seen in a dream,—
Vainly I try to keep you. How the sky,
A great blue wind, with a gigantic laugh,
Scorns us apart like chaff.
Like a bird blown to sea am I.

O let us hold, amid these immensities,
The blinding blaze of the hostile infinite,
To the one clear phrase we knew and still may
 know:
Walls rise daily and darkly between us
But love has seen us,
Wherever we go love too must go.

Beautiful, twilight, mysterious, bird-haunted land
Seen from the ship, with the far pale shore of
 sand,

And the blue folds of hills inviting the stars to
    rest,
Though I shall never set foot there, nor explore
    you,
Nor hear your angelus of bells about me, I shall
    adore you
And know you still the best.

VI

Let me suppose your ghost sits here beside me—
You, who are living still, but dead for me—
For friendly talk.　And let me suppose you say,—
Clasping long hands together in a familiar way,
Giving your profile, only, for me to see,—

The charming wisdoms, exquisitely said,
That often have made me lift in delight my head
As for a glimpse of heights, in the sky, unknown;
O let me suppose, for this deliciousness,
A quiet room, and we two there alone,

Facing in dusk the mirror's watery stare
At the pale panelled wall, and the quiet air
Which yet not even a candle-flame shall fever;
With two blue vases above us, and no clock
Whose febrile insistent tiny voice might mock
The illusion that we sit here so forever:

Only your beauty, and my agitation,
To make, of the tranquil scene, a situation.
O then perhaps at laſt I would say to you
The words I have often implored myself to say:
'Let us no longer try what wit can do!

'But see, with the poor courage we command,
Sadly, profoundly, without a tremor of hand
Or faltering of the long delicious gaze,
The wretched beauty our hopeless love has given;
And speak at laſt, in silence, the perfeȼt praise

'So long withheld! O let us together move
Unmoving, in the rich knowledge of our love,
Touching—not hand to hand, since that's for-
        bidden,—
But wing to wing, in our full consciousness;
Stirring the luminous twilight to confess
That love like ours no longer can be hidden.'

Thus let us sit, in silence, without motion,
While the moment shakes bright leaves above us;
        then,
I would have you say, laying aside your wit,
Quite simply: 'It began, in such a way,
That afternoon—do you recall the day?—
We walked together!' . . . A pause, then, ex-
        quisite,

Infinite, azure, deep as the world is deep;
And I, like one arousing himself from sleep,
Would answer: 'And I too, that afternoon,
Turning toward you, to tell you of a tree
Which held, among its half-fledged leaves, the
     moon,

'Suddenly felt your beauty over me
Falling like light. My eyes filled. I could see
Nothing, thenceforth, but you' . . . And silence
     again;
While, for a moment infinite in duration,
Our troubled eyes, across our separation,
Found, beneath our blessing, infinite pain.

VII

Why is it, as I enter at last the panelled room,
And pause, having opened the door,
And turning my eyes from wall to wall in the
     gloom
Find all as it was before,—

Something, a slow, grave, passionless wave of
     grief,
So whelms me in silence there,
That I listen, like one who loses his only belief,
In vain to the voiceless air?

Did I expect, in my absence, that you had come—
You, or a sign from you—
To lend a voice to a beauty that else was dumb?
But alas, there is nothing new,

The room is the same, the same, there has been
no change,
The table, the chairs are the same,
Nothing has altered, nothing is singing and
strange,
No hover of light or flame;

And the walls have not, as in an illusion of spring,
Blossomed, nor the oaken chair
Put forth pale leaves, nor is there a bird to sing
In the mystically widened air.

Yet if you had come, and stood for an instant
dreaming,
And thought my name and gone,
Leaving behind you hardly a stir of seeming,
I should no less have known;

For this would have been no longer the hated
room
Whose walls imprison me now,

But the infinite heavens, and one white bough in
    bloom,
And a bird to sing on the bough.

VIII

Dante, walking once by the muddy river,
Watched the inscrutable angel pass him by,
Shutting her flower-like heart. . . . He turned
    his torment
To torture of a world let slowly die.

But I shall hide my torment like a fever
Within my breast, rejoicing when it feeds
Upon my heart; then only being certain
I live, when most my weak heart burns and
    bleeds.

Singular ending! brutal, perverse, unlooked for.
There, by the river, had I turned my head
To the shy doubtful exquisite smile you proffered
I should not now so slowly, like one dead,

Move as among the damned, unknown, unseeing,
Crying to heaven with lips that make no sound:
Heavily yearning downward, as the clay does,
Hapless and hopeless, parted from the ground.

There is nothing moving there, in that desert of
    silence,
Nothing living there, not even a blade of grass.
The morning there is as silent as the evening,
The nights and days with an equal horror pass.

Nothing moving except the cold, slow shadow
Thrown on sand by a boulder, or by the cliff
Whose rock not even a lichen comes to cover,
To hide—from what?—time's ancient hieroglyph.

The sun, at noon, sings like a flaming cymbal
Above that waste: but the waste makes no reply.
In all that desolation of rock and gravel
There is no water, no answer to the sky.

Sometimes, perhaps, from other lands more
    happy,
A faint wind, slow, exhausted, ventures there,
And loses itself in silence, like a music.
And then—who knows?—beneath that alien air,

Which moves mysteriously as memory over
Forlorn abysms and peaks of stone and sand,
Ghosts of delight awake for a shining moment,
And all is troubled, and that desolate land

Remembers grass and flowers, and birds that sang
    there
Their miracles of song in lovely trees,
And waters that poured, or stood, in dreaming
    azure,
Praising the sky. Perhaps once more it sees

The rose, the moon, the pool, in the blue evening,
And knows that silence in which one bird will
    sing
Slowly and sleepily his praise of gardens.
Perhaps once more, for a moment, it remembers
    Spring.

X

HE

Say that we move together, sorrowful and silent,
To one high window which out-tops the sky,
And see, in the dusk, not even the crests of beech-
    trees,
Not even, in the wide blue, the flash of a bird.
And there, as if we stood alone on a headland,
Facing, in the long sunlight, all the sea,
Search the blue twilight of infinity;
And do not say a word.

[115]

PRIAPUS AND THE POOL

SHE

You are romantic, you exaggerate;
It is a balcony on which we stand.

HE

This much you grant: we stand there so together.
What can it matter, if, questioning thus the star-
    light,
We do not trouble to regard each other?
Think what you will: be but a consciousness
Of night, and music that is sentimental—
Night, and the balustrade beneath your hand.
Say that you do not love me, never loved,
Know naught of love, nor think it worth the
    knowing.
Yet lies the infinite with all its azure
Like a vast sea around us, glares us up
For a long moment into terrible nothing.
And we are frightened; and we stand and stare
Into that shining silence, and are glad,
As lovers are, to feel the other there.

SHE

That is not love that takes but what it finds
In a dark hour. If frightened here, we cling,
It is not love, it is a transient thing.

Say afterward: We did not love, but only
Together turned for one inscrutable moment,
Held in the hand of the infinite, being lonely.
This is an intimacy we shall forget.
We shall be strangers yet.

HE

It is the moment in which the infinite
Closes about us. Turn, therefore, to me.
Call it what name you will, brief let it be;
Be conscious, if you must, of loneliness
And little else: but if this is not love,
Then nothing is. The stars, the night, the music
Eddy away beneath us and are gone.
We stand here. We are living. We are alone.

XI

The mirror says: Condole not too profoundly
With the pale thing you see yourself to be.
Do not recall that dead men sleep so soundly,
Nor wanly see

The sad procession passing, as a symbol
Of your so-much-to-be-pitied state of mind.
What you would shut in a coffin is too nimble
To be confined.

PRIAPUS AND THE POOL

Look! as you search these depths, gleefully seeing
The atomy spectral coffin darkly pass,
Far off flashes a gesture of someone fleeing;
Across the glass,

In that small circle of shadow (which I show you
Your introspective eye is) goes the ghost
Of a delightful grief which seems to know you
Yet counts you lost.

She turns her dark young beautiful head toward
      you,
Sombrely looks at you, and, least foreseen,
Dazzlingly smiles at you, as if to reward you—
Most generous queen!—

For the one word not said, the light betrayed not;
And turning upon the dusk is vaguely gone
Out of that world of yours she sought not, made
      not,
Nor would have known.

O rain of light! Ten times a day you stand here
To watch that brown-eyed ghost of delight es-
      cape,
Happy in knowing you now forever command
      here
That lovely shape.

XII

I shut my eyes, I try to remember you.
But as a diver plunging down through sunlight
To meet his azure shadow on the wide water
Shatters through it and is gone,
Thus I, coming suddenly upon your ghost,
See it but cannot grasp it: it is lost.
I stand in the dark and call you. I am alone.

Come to me: stand before me: turn your head
Sharply against the light: put forth one hand
Holding an amber bead: then let it fall.
Say 'It is nothing!' Slowly rise and move,
Darkened, against the open window; against the
    wall
Pause, with the sombre gesture that I love,
And slowly say, 'I do not understand.'

How I have seen you! How I have drunk of
    you!
Now, when I most would have you, you escape.
Thus is your mouth? or thus? I do not know.
But see, I ignore you now, bewildering shape,
Flee in the darkness from you. . . . And you
    come
Laughing before me, saying, 'I love you so!'

XIII

Now over the grass you come,
Gravely you come with a slow step
Into the azure world I call my heart:
Tardily you approach me.

Butterflies of the sun flicker about you—
Who could have foreseen it?
Moths of the moon at your finger-tips
Melt like flakes of snow.

Is it not too late that you come?
Are you not merely a ghost?
Behold, before you once speak my name,
Wind whirls us apart like leaves.

Never again, after this dream, shall I have peace.
In my heart is nothing but the crying of snow.
The grass over which I seek you is white with
    frost.
You have left upon it no footstep.

I place my most secret thought
Like a bough of magnolia
Where perhaps you will find it and remember.
It withers, and you do not come.

XIV

Suddenly, as I gaze at the sombre land in the
      picture,
The bridge, the enchanted stream, the long, long
      watery plain,
And the dark wood, and the small far houses,
      and the blue hills
Flashing like dolphins under a light like rain;

Look! The picture has opened! the sounds come
      in,
Broad, rich streaming, in the late light of the sun,
The whole wide land is a flood of mysterious
      sound! . . .
O this is the land where you have gone,

Your voice floats up to me from that bridge, I
      hear
The tiny words out of dusk like a gnat-song
      come—
'Stay! stay where you are! You will be happier
      there!
I will at last, perhaps, come home!'

O voice, crying the ineffable, face invisible,
Beauty intangibly gone like a tracery out of the
      sky!

Come back! . . . But the window closes. Bridge,
    stream, houses, hills,
Are silent. Small is the picture. None stirs in
    the world save I.

XV

There was an island in the sea
That out of immortal chaos reared
Towers of topaz, trees of pearl,
For maidens adored and warriors feared.

Long ago it sunk in the sea;
And now, a thousand fathoms deep,
Sea-worms above it whirl their lamps,
Crabs on the pale mosaic creep.

Voyagers over that haunted sea
Hear from the waters under the keel
A sound that is not wave or foam;
Nor do they only hear, but feel

The timbers quiver, as eerily comes
Up from the dark an elfin singing
Of voices happy as none can be,
And bells an ethereal anthem ringing.

[122]

Thereafter, where they go or come,
They will be silent; they have heard
Out of the infinite of the soul
An incommunicable word;

Thereafter, they are as lovers who
Over an infinite brightness lean:
'It is Atlantis!', all their speech;
'To lost Atlantis have we been.'

XVI

See, as the carver carves a rose,
A wing, a toad, a serpent's eye,
In cruel granite, to disclose
The soft things that in hardness lie,

So this one, taking up his heart,
Which time and change had made a stone,
Carved out of it with dolorous art,
Labouring yearlong and alone,

The thing there hidden—rose, toad, wing?
A frog's hand on a lily pad?
Bees in a cobweb—? No such thing!
A girl's head was the thing he had,

[123]

Small, shapely, richly crowned with hair,
Drowsy, with eyes half closed, as they
Looked through you and beyond you, clear
To something farther than Cathay:

Saw you, yet counted you not worth
The seeing, thinking all the while
How, flower-like, beauty comes to birth;
And thinking this, began to smile.

Medusa! For she could not see
The world she turned to stone and ash.
Only herself she saw, a tree
That flowered beneath a lightning-flash.

Thus dreamed her face—a lovely thing,
To worship, weep for, or to break.
Better to carve a claw, a wing,
Or, if the heart provide, a snake.

XVII

Fade, then,—die, depart, and come no more—
You, whose beauty I abhor—
Out of my brain
Take back your voice that lodges there in pain,
Tear out your thousand golden roots
That thrust their tentacles in my heart
But bear no fruits.

[124]

Now like an exquisite but sterile tree
Your beauty grows in me
And feeds on light
Its lifted arms of leaves and blossoms white.
Come birds, come bees,
And marry flower with flower that it may bear
Like other trees.

Or else let hatred like a lightning come,
And flash, and strike it numb,
And strew on rock
These singing leaves, that, singing, seem to mock.
Thus let my heart once more be naked stone,
Bare under wind and hard with grief,
And leave not in a single crevice
A single leaf.

XVIII

First the white crocus, and then the purple; then
    the rain
Daylong and nightlong lashing the bitter garden,
Blurring, by day, the light on the window-pane,
Beating by night with talons. And after the rain
A cold clear day, no crocus left; and shrill
In the high cold poplar a ruffled robin singing;
And, in the cold grass, one clear daffodil,
Downcast, in pale light swinging.

First the red tulip, and then the white; and then
    the wind
Daylong and nightlong curving long poplar
    boughs
To green sonorous arcs against blue heaven,
The new leaves baffled. And after that carouse
A steamy fog that clings to tree and bush
And hides the shattered tulip. Sad is he
Who slowly at daybreak walks in the bitter gar-
    den
That ruin to see.

A day? A year? They come, they go, like
    weather,
Give leaves or take them. Here alone I move
Slowly in this small garden, deeply regarding
The flower, the tree, the grass, the weed, I love;
Dig here, plant there, or with a sickle cut
The too-thick clover. But whether there or here,
Have with me, for my calendar, crocus, tulip,
Daffodil, robin; and they say 'a year.'

Doomed brightly, darkly doomed, doomed from
    the first!
And sleep becomes but the gateway to a dream
Of a wise intimacy I never knew.
Now must I seek you in a garden gleam

PRIAPUS AND THE POOL

Of tulip petals fallen, crocus withered,
Lilacs in bud, a sickle's edge. At night
I dream we walk and talk beneath low lime-trees
Palely in flower, as under an arch of light;

The petals, greener than golden, fall or hover,
Blow, twirl, float, and litter with flame the
    ground,
The air is alight with pollen. And there we loiter,
Laughing deliciously, and hear the slow sound
Of our two voices, happily weaving together
A harmony simple in seeming but strange beyond
    thought:
The words we say are beautiful, but have no
    meaning;
And as I wake and repeat them, they are nought.

First the white crocus, and then the purple; then
    the rain
Drawing its grey diagonals across the garden,
Wrinkling, by day, the light on the window-pane,
Scratching by night with claws. And after the
    rain
The unfamiliar silence in which we wake,
And seek, no longer storm-and-fever-tossed,
In the cool dark for a pale brightness dreamed of:
And find, at last, the memory of something lost.

XIX

Bitter nasturtium, pale pink phlox, scarlet william
Wrung like blood-drops from the suffering earth,
Dance in the southwest wind in the lamentable
  garden:
They are poor words to stammer your worth!—
Or curses for you; or, in the colourless moon-
  light,
Black cries and imprecations; with slow hands
I tear the offending heads off, strip them, smell
  them,
And crush them under my heel against harsh
  sands.

Come out of the earth like these with earth upon
  you,
Hands soiled with loam, lips flecked, the sunset
  cheek
Fouled with black webs and leaves, and the rich
  hair
Inhabited by spiders. I would speak
Not then as one fool to another babbles,
But with a natural tongue, as leaf to leaf
Nasturtium touches phlox in the dewy morning,
And the strong stems, growing together, know
  no grief.

[128]

But you are poisonous, dyed deep in death,
Black at the heart! Grow here, and you will
    spread
A low rank mist that, snake-like amid the flowers,
Will coil, delighting them, and leave them dead.
But ah, to have you like that snake pass by,
Drawing against my palms your viscous scales
Of venomous colours and translucent brightness!
    There
My blossom falls upon you, my strong leaf fails.

XX

You are indifferent: think not of me:
Lead a wild life of days strangely begot,
Days that rise from a different source than mine,
Days that come up like giants out of the sea.
How should you think of me?
How should you think of one you never knew,
Who never disclosed his heart to you?

Now to a picture stoop you, now to an image,
Now to an idol you abase your knees,
Walk in a dim light praying, touch your heart
With tears of imagined gods. You sigh for
    these,
O foolish one! and seas

Send up star-bearing giants of days to you,
Rich in all lovely things; you knew

What words I said to you by a tall window
Where the sunlight came in mottled through a
    vine:
But you forget them. And the blue giants come
Bearing vast days how different from mine,
Globed, perfect, light as wine,
In which young gods like tyrannous dancers move
To music that is the voice of love.

Sleep, if you remember me not in waking; dream
Of one word lightly and profoundly said
By him you had forgotten, whose dim face
Is dimmer than faces of remembered dead:
Half wake, and turn your head,
Wondering who he was and what he meant.
Then I shall be content.

XXI

See now, after all these days I have the strength,
Yes, now at length,
To drive you forth, pale ghost! Ah, now I come
With flowers for whips and my dull heart for
    drum

And flog you out of the shadow of my brain,
Laughing whip you with flowers from vein to
     vein,
Shout, should a petal
Upon your rich hair settle,
Care not if red stains mark, or bruises dark,
Your flesh that was the integument of you,
Heed not the imagined cries,
Nor tears, if tears you have, that light your eyes.

Go, come not hither again, proud sorceress,
Idolatrous self-worshipper!
Into the tabernacle of my heart and brain
Come not again.
For now I rid me of the imperfect you,
You, halt when you would dance; you, dumb
     when you would sing,
You, dark when starlike you would shine!
Now a more perfect idol shall be mine,
Now the bright goddess will I bring,
Not garlanded with flowers nor bright with gems
Nor gay with diadems,
But her more holy who is born of dream
And who like light itself shall gleam.

She whom a vision shapes
Obeys not death nor change, nor ever escapes

Her worshipper, though dull of heart he be.
So now I make her
Out of the finest azure and pale fire,
To worship, not desire,
And none but I shall take her.
You were the last and greatest of those few
In whose imperfect flesh I thought I knew
Beauty: it burned in you
Briefly and brightly.
Now that it dims, in pity I whip you forth,
Scourge you with flowers that it may hurt you
    less—
For you have still your loveliness—
And dream the dream that I shall worship nightly.

O come not, lest against this perfect tree
You, who were once so dear to me,
And still, alas, perhaps too dear,
Must by my zealous hands be crucified,
Nailed with strong hands against that tree
    immortal:
To mark the portal
Wherethrough, no longer human,
At last, at last all flesh-forgetful,
I pass, to make a dream my bride.
Come not! Lest when I find you,
Weeping I bind you,

Bandage your eyes, not lest they see
But lest they injure me:
Chain the strong hands and feet that were my joy
Not that I hate them but lest they destroy:
And dumbly watch you die, to praise that beauty
To which henceforth, I swear it by my love,
I owe all duty.

XXII

Madonna of the eyes wide open, the white hands
    slender,
Madonna of the young smile tremulous and
    tender,
And the dark hair turned in wings aside
From the brow white and wide:

Madonna tall, standing as one who listens
To a far grave music, music that murmurs and
    glistens
With a secret perhaps unguessed
And comes to rest:

Madonna tall, standing as one who lingers
To hear a melody rise from invisible fingers,
Fingers invisible to me,
Who only see

[133]

How, in your eyes, the light for a moment changes,
Darkening to an abysm which estranges
Infinities apart
Me from your heart:

Madonna of the woman's body, the face of a child,
Madonna of whom only the lips have ever smiled,
Flowers to conceal the secret tear
None see or hear:

Not of the rays of the moon, could they be cloven,
Could such a beauty of flesh as yours be woven;
Not with so subtle a mesh
As the clear flesh

Which the soft wandering dream of you keeps
   bright
As with the singing imprisoned bird of light:
Not out of the beauty of dust or air
Comes aught so fair.

I stand bewildered, I stand in silence before you,
Knowing only the one thing, that I adore you;
Fearing so much that speech
Will never reach,

PRIAPUS AND THE POOL

Nor these hands touch you, nor my terrible love
    arouse you,
Nor the dark house of the earth I inhabit house
    you;
O better it were in sorrow to cry
To a birdless sky

Than with a voice or silence to importune
You, silent, inscrutable, as to the sea the dune,
Which gives to the sea's hands
Not self but sands.

It is not you I touch! . . . O strange cool being,
Even in whose laughter falls the shadow of
    someone fleeing,
Bewildered denial in the caress,
No in the yes,

How shall we love? For we are worlds asunder,
Between us the demon chasms wail and thunder.
Ah, terrible destiny
If you should be

Agonized victim of the perverse gods who shape
    you,
Destined forever to see your soul escape you,
As one who remembers, yet remembers not,
Something forgot:

Desiring to give to me, to see me live,
Your soul, yet having, alas, no soul to give;
Desiring to give, that you
Might so live too;

And waiting thus in a tragic dumb confusion,
Weaving a shining mystery of your seclusion,
Miraculous beauty of mask;
Yet when I ask

For more than the mask, for the secret light
    behind,
Confessing—ah, what horror!—that you are
    blind.
Here, then, our destiny takes us
And binds and breaks us.

IMPROVISATIONS: LIGHTS AND SNOW

IMPROVISATIONS: LIGHTS AND SNOW

I

The girl in the room beneath
Before going to bed
Strums on a mandolin
The three simple tunes she knows.
How inadequate they are to tell what her heart
  feels!
When she has finished them several times
She thrums the strings aimlessly with her finger-
  nails
And smiles, and thinks happily of many things.

II

I stood for a long while before the shop-window
Looking at the blue butterflies embroidered on
  tawny silk.
The building was a tower before me,
Time was loud behind me,
Sun went over the housetops and dusty trees;
And there they were, glistening, brilliant, motion-
  less,

Stitched in a golden sky
By yellow patient fingers long since turned to dust.

III

The first bell is silver,
And breathing darkness I think only of the long
    scythe of time.
The second bell is crimson,
And I think of a holiday night, with rockets
Furrowing the sky with red, and a soft shatter of
    stars.
The third bell is saffron and slow,
And I behold a long sunset over the sea
With wall on wall of castled cloud and glittering
    balustrades.
The fourth bell is colour of bronze,
I walk by a frozen lake in the dun light of dusk:
Muffled crackings run in the ice,
Trees creak, birds fly.
The fifth bell is cold clear azure,
Delicately tinged with green:
One golden star hangs melting in it,
And towards this, sleepily, I go.
The sixth bell is as if a pebble
Had been dropped into a deep sea far above
    me . . .
Rings of sound ebb slowly into the silence.

IV

On the day when my uncle and I drove to the
  cemetery,
Rain rattled on the roof of the carriage;
And talking constrainedly of this and that
We refrained from looking at the child's coffin
  on the seat before us.
When we reached the cemetery
We found that the thin snow on the grass
Was already darkly transparent with rain;
And boards had been laid upon it
That we might walk without wetting our feet.

V

When I was a boy, and saw bright rows of icicles
In many lengths along a wall
I was disappointed to find
That I could not play music upon them:
I ran my hand lightly across them
And they fell, tinkling.
I tell you this, young man, so that your expecta-
  tions of life
Will not be too great.

VI

It is now two hours since I left you,
And the perfume of your hands is still on my
  hands.

And though since then
I have looked at the stars, walked in the cold
    blue streets,
And heard the dead leaves blowing over the
    ground
Under the trees,
I still remember the sound of your laughter.
How will it be, lady, when there is none to
    remember you
Even as long as this?
Will the dust braid your hair?

VII

The day opens with the brown light of snowfall
And past the window snowflakes fall and fall.
I sit in my chair all day and work and work
Measuring words against each other.
I open the piano and play a tune
But find it does not say what I feel,
I grow tired of measuring words against each
    other,
I grow tired of these four walls,
And I think of you, who write me that you have
    just had a daughter
And named her after your first sweetheart,
And you, who break your heart, far away,

In the confusion and savagery of a long war,
And you who, worn by the bitterness of winter,
Will soon go south.
The snowflakes fall almost straight in the brown
    light
Past my window,
And a sparrow finds refuge on my window-ledge.
This alone comes to me out of the world outside
As I measure word with word.

VIII

Many things perplex me and leave me troubled,
Many things are locked away in the white book
    of stars
Never to be opened by me.
The starred leaves are silently turned,
And the mooned leaves;
And as they are turned, fall the shadows of life
    and death.
Perplexed and troubled,
I light a small light in a small room,
The lighted walls come closer to me,
The familiar pictures are clear.
I sit in my favourite chair and turn in my mind
The tiny pages of my own life, whereon so little
    is written,

And hear at the eastern window the pressure of
    a long wind, coming
From I know not where.

How many times have I sat here,
How many times will I sit here again,
Thinking these same things over and over in
    solitude
As a child says over and over
The first word he has learned to say.

IX

This girl gave her heart to me,
And this, and this.
This one looked at me as if she loved me,
And silently walked away.
This one I saw once and loved, and saw her never
    again.

Shall I count them for you upon my fingers?
Or like a priest solemnly sliding beads?
Or pretend they are roses, pale pink, yellow, and
    white,
And arrange them for you in a wide bowl
To be set in sunlight?
See how nicely it sounds as I count them for you—
'This girl gave her heart to me
And this, and this' . . . !

And nevertheless my heart breaks when I think
    of them,
When I think their names,
And how, like leaves, they have changed and
    blown
And will lie at last, forgotten,
Under the snow.

x

It is night-time, and cold, and snow is falling,
And no wind grieves the walls.
In the small world of light around the arc-lamp
A swarm of snowflakes falls and falls.
The street grows silent.   The last stranger passes.
The sound of his feet, in the snow, is indistinct.

What forgotten sadness is it, on a night like this,
Takes possession of my heart?
Why do I think of a camellia tree in a southern
    garden,
With pink blossoms among dark leaves,
Standing, surprised, in the snow?
Why do I think of spring?

The snowflakes, helplessly veering,
Fall silently past my window;

[145]

They come from darkness and enter darkness.
What is it in my heart is surprised and bewildered
Like that camellia tree,
Beautiful still in its glittering anguish?
And spring so far away!

XI

As I walked through the lamplit gardens,
On the thin white crust of snow,
So intensely was I thinking of my misfortune,
So clearly were my eyes fixed
On the face of this grief which has come to me,
That I did not notice the beautiful pale colouring
Of lamplight on the snow;
Nor the interlaced long blue shadows of trees;

And yet these things were there,
And the white lamps and orange lamps, and lamps
    of lilac were there,
As I have seen them so often before;
As they will be so often again
Long after my grief is forgotten.

And still, though I know this, and say this, it
    cannot console me.

XII

How many times have we been interrupted
Just as I was about to make up a story for you!

One time it was because we suddenly saw a firefly
Lighting his green lantern among the boughs of a
      fir-tree.
Marvellous! Marvellous! He is making for
      himself
A little tent of light in the darkness!
And one time it was because we saw a lilac
      lightning flash
Run wrinkling into the blue top of the mountain,—
We heard boulders of thunder rolling down upon
      us
And the plat-plat of drops on the window,
And we ran to watch the rain
Charging in wavering white clouds across the long
      grass of the field!
Or at other times it was because we saw a star
Slipping easily out of the sky and falling, far off,
Among pine-dark hills;
Or because we found a crimson eft
Darting in the cold grass!

These things interrupted us and left us wondering;
And the stories, whatever they might have been,
Were never told.
A fairy, binding a daisy down and laughing?
A golden-haired princess caught in a cobweb?
A love-story of long ago?

Some day, just as we are beginning again,
Just as we blow the first sweet note,
Death itself will interrupt us.

XIII

My heart is an old house, and in that forlorn old
  house,
In the very centre, dark and forgotten,
Is a locked room where an enchanted princess
Lies sleeping.
But sometimes, in that dark house,
As if almost from the stars, far away,
Sounds whisper in that secret room—
Faint voices, music, a dying trill of laughter?
And suddenly, from her long sleep,
The beautiful princess awakes and dances.

Who is she? I do not know.
Why does she dance? Do not ask me!—
Yet to-day, when I saw you,
When I saw your eyes troubled with the trouble
  of happiness,
And your mouth trembling into a smile,
And your fingers put shyly forward,—
Softly, in that room,
The little princess arose
And danced;

And as she danced the old house gravely trembled
With its vague and delicious secret.

XIV

Like an old tree uprooted by the wind
And flung down cruelly
With roots bared to the sun and stars
And limp leaves brought to earth—
Torn from its house—
So do I seem to myself
When you have left me.

XV

The music of the morning is red and warm;
Snow lies against the walls;
And on the sloping roof in the yellow sunlight
Pigeons huddle against the wind.
The music of the evening is attenuated and thin—
The moon seen through a wave by a mermaid;
The crying of a violin.

Far down there, far down where the river turns
     to the west,
The delicate lights begin to twinkle
On the dusky arches of the bridge:
In the green sky a long cloud,
A smouldering wave of smoky crimson,

Breaks in the freezing wind: and above it,
    unabashed,
Remote, untouched, fierily palpitant,
Sings the first star.

NOTE: The arrangement of the poems in this book is roughly chronological. The majority of the blank verse poems in the first section were written in 1924. Exceptions to this are *Psychomachia* and *Poverty Grass* (both early 1922); *Exile, Seven Twilights,* and *Samadhi* (1921); and *Tetélestai* (1918). *Priapus and the Pool* was written in 1920 and 1921; *Improvisations* in 1917.

Samadhi, Poverty Grass, and *Tetélestai* are parts of a longer poem. I print them here because they have appeared separately in periodicals and anthologies, and because the completion and publication of the parent poem is problematic.

Priapus and the Pool was first published in 1922 by the Dunster House Bookshop, Cambridge, in a limited edition printed by Mr. Bruce Rogers. The present version is a slightly revised one, and three poems have been omitted.